**Second Edition Revised and Updated**

# THE 16% SOLUTION

## How to Get High Interest Rates in a Low Interest World with Tax Lien Certificates

## Joel S. Moskowitz, J.D.

Andrews McMeel
PUBLISHING®

Andrews McMeel Publishing
a division of Andrews McMeel Universal
1130 Walnut Street, Kansas City, Missouri 64106

17 18 19 20 21 QGR 11 10 9 8 7

Library of Congress Cataloging-in-Publication Data

Moskowitz, Joel S.
 The 16% solution : how to get high interest rates in a low-interest world with tax lien certificates / Joel S. Moskowitz. – Rev. ed.
     p. cm.
 ISBN: 978-0-7407-6962-7
 1.  Real estate investment. 2.  Tax lien certificates. 3.  Real estate investment–United States. 4.  Tax lien certificates–United States. I. Title. II. Title: Sixteen percent solution.

 HD1382.5.M69 2009
 332.63'24–dc22

                              2008053750

ATTENTION: SCHOOLS AND BUSINESSES
Andrews McMeel books are available at quantity discounts with bulk purchase for educational, business, or sales promotional use. For information, please e-mail the Andrews McMeel Publishing Special Sales Department: specialsales@amuniversal.com.

# Contents

# PREFACE TO THE ORIGINAL EDITION

Like millions of others, you are probably wondering where to put your money in these low interest times. Money market funds, banks, and savings and loans are paying less than 5% interest. After taxes and inflation, a 5% return leaves you with nothing at all.

Eager for higher yields, you may be considering joining millions of others who are rushing into an already overpriced stock market. Or you may be considering buying bonds, options, or more exotic instruments that may one day cost you some or most of your principal.

There is an alternative. An investment that will allow you to reap ultra-high yields. An investment that will allow you to sleep at night. An investment you can get into with very little money. An investment that is fun. I wrote this book to introduce you to that investment, known as tax lien certificates.

Tax lien certificates are not some new invention of a brokerage. They are issued by over 1,000 local governments in a majority of states. Banks, savings and loans, and many knowledgeable investors hold them. Now it's your turn to find out about them, and your turn to profit from them.

Frankly, I'm excited for you. You are in for a wonderful, profitable discovery, and I am delighted to be your guide and companion.

Joel S. Moskowitz

# FOREWORD

As this revised edition of *The 16% Solution* goes to press, it's a dangerous financial world out there. Counting inflation, the average stock has lost over 50% of its value in a few weeks. Those seeking safety in U.S. Treasury bonds are realizing minimal returns on their investments. Those who hoped that their homes would be a haven for their money have watched that investment turn to dust.

By contrast, tax lien certificates are untouched as an island of safe, high-yield returns. Tax liens don't depend on a strong economy or the success of a rescue plan to make money. They don't depend on consumer spending holding up. There is no need to take a wild and dangerous roller-coaster ride to reap ample returns. And your capital is secured and guaranteed by the state government where you invest. This revised edition of *The 16% Solution* comes 15 years after the first. There have been many changes in the world of tax liens in that time.

First, now there's the Internet. When this book originally appeared, most of us had never even heard of the Internet. Today, you can get information online about tax lien sales in almost all counties. In most counties, you can find out what tax liens are for sale. In many counties, you can do research on the properties, and in some cases, you can do *all* your research online. Nowadays, in many counties, you can even *buy* your tax liens online; you don't even have to show up in the state! (I should add here that I recommend you check out properties in person; that's the only way you'll know whether a house has burned down or been washed away in a flood or whether any of a thousand other things has occurred that can affect the value of the property.)

Second, there are now TV infomercials and seminars touting tax lien investing as a surefire way to get rich quick. They show you pictures of lovely homes that someone got for "pennies on the dollar" by buying tax liens on the property and later foreclosing. Their examples could well be true. But it's also true that I could introduce you to a waitress who made $1 million by betting $1 on the lottery. Such examples distort reality; the truth is that it's highly unlikely you'll ever get a house by investing in tax liens. I've never gotten one, and nobody I know has ever gotten one. What you *will* get with tax liens is super-high interest combined with safety.

Third, there have been innumerable changes in the laws and procedures of states and counties that offer tax lien certificates. This new edition will update you extensively on these changes. I would like to acknowledge the assistance of Linda Rosencrance in researching them.

The world of tax lien certificates is an exciting and rewarding place. I remain privileged to serve as your guide.

Joel Moskowitz, J.D.

# Why You Need Tax Lien Certificates

## CHAPTER 1

# What Are Tax Lien Certificates?

## A TALE OF TWO BROTHERS

*Andy's heart sank. When he retired, his retirement nest egg of $100,000 was earning him 8% in the money market. That extra $667 each month, supplementing his Social Security, went a long way toward making his retirement comfortable. But these last years, he had been watching his interest rates steadily drop, until this last month he earned just $220 in interest.*

*Andy had so many plans: a trip with Carol to visit the kids in California, adding on a guest room for visits from the grandchildren, buying a small boat to go fishing on the lake. Now he and his wife would have to dip deeper into their principal each month just to keep up their present lifestyle. And that would hurt their future income. He could see in the distance a time when their money was gone before they were.*

*Andy's brother Jay, on the other hand, put his money into Arizona tax lien certificates. Although they had saved a similar amount from their jobs, Jay's nest egg had been growing and compounding at a steady 16% for many years. At retirement, Jay had $325,000, all of which was still making 16% despite what was happening to interest rates in the rest of the economy. Jay was raking in an additional $50,000 a year! With that money, he and his wife were traveling and had just bought a rental house in the Caribbean.*

Today, you will have to search for a certificate of deposit paying more than 5%. Although some experts believe that rates will rise in future years, others observe that today's rates are more in line with those that have existed during most of this century.

This presents you with a major problem, particularly if you live on or intend to live on the income produced by your savings.

Today, you will have to search for a certificate of deposit paying more than 5%.

If you are like
most people, you
are struggling,
without much
success, to get the
yield back into
your savings.

If you are like most people, you are struggling, without much success, to get the yield back into your savings. The places to which you are turning are not producing much relief.

As of this writing, the following are typical yields on common investments:

| | |
|---|---|
| 5-year Treasury Note | 2.95% |
| 10-year Treasury Bonds | 3.77% |
| High Grade Corporate Bonds | 3.80% |
| Money Market Funds | 2.50% |
| Utility Stocks | 5.8% |
| 1-year Certificates of Deposit | 2.75% |

Several of these investments present peculiar risks. In chapter 3, we will consider in detail how to compare investments and combine them into a complete strategy. For the moment, we need to reflect that, particularly after taxes and inflation, these yields are very low.

## A TALE OF TWO CITIES

FREEMART, CONNECTICUT: *Freemart was in trouble. Maybe not as much trouble as it had been in when the state was forced to step in and guarantee a $35 million deficit bond. Still, the bond money was gone, and this year the city faced a $20 million deficit in its $320 million budget.*

*Freemart had just elected Joseph Jones to be its mayor. Looking over the city's financial statement, he noticed that $9.25 million in property taxes was owed, a number that was growing during the recession. He and the city's finance director went before the state's review board to propose that Freemart be the first city in Connecticut to sell tax lien certificates. Jones explained that if the liens were sold, "we're going to see a number of individuals who have used the city as their bank say, 'Wait a minute, they're getting serious.'"*

METROPOLE: *By the end of its 1991 fiscal year, Metropole was owed more than $500 million in property taxes. A group of real estate professionals, naming themselves "Collect," complained that the failure of some people to pay their taxes meant that taxes would have to be raised* *on the rest of the community to make up the shortfall. It proposed that the sale of tax lien certificates would allow a property tax cut. This, in turn, would encourage businesses to stay in the city. Furthermore, said Collect, getting those dollars into the city's pocket would help pay for vital city services.*

*The property owners, they noted, would owe exactly the same penalty anyway. What difference did it make if they owed it to the city or to an investor?*

*Not everyone was pleased with the idea. Some officials thought that the city should continue to earn the 18% penalty rather than pay it to investors. Others replied that the city was very slow to collect, if it collected at all. One attorney was concerned for his clients because a private investor would obtain the delinquent property more promptly than the city.*

## TAX LIEN CERTIFICATES: A SOLUTION FOR TWO PROBLEMS

One side effect of the recent recession and housing crash is that many property owners, who often are not paying their mortgages, cannot or will not pay their property taxes either. Local governments, which depend on those taxes to provide services, find it difficult to budget, or even to function, if the taxes owed do not arrive on time.

They can, and do, assess high penalties for failure to pay, and they have the power to foreclose on the property. The problem with these solutions is that while they are being pursued, the government is without its money.

In ideal circumstances, the local government would rather collect and keep the penalty itself. However, it is in the same situation as the delinquent taxpayers, who, in ideal times, would rather pay the tax and be spared the penalty. Local governments are not in the lending business, and, strapped for cash to provide immediate essential services, they do not have money to lend.

More than 1,000 local governments in 23 states are already issuing tax lien certificates. These certificates solve the government's need for a predictable, adequate cash flow while solving the investor's need for a safe, high rate of interest. The government does not mind that you're getting the high rate of interest because

Local governments, which depend on those taxes to provide services, find it difficult to budget, or even to function, if the taxes owed do not arrive on time.

In ideal circumstances, the local government would rather collect and keep the penalty itself. However, it is in the same situation as the delinquent taxpayers, who, in ideal times, would rather pay the tax and be spared the penalty.

By stepping into the shoes of the government, you have a right to get the government's interest and have the same rights over the property that the government would have.

the government is not paying it. The property owners in the community who are paying taxes are thankful that their taxes will not be raised to make up the shortfall. Even the property owners who are delinquent do not care whether you get this interest because they would have to pay the same penalty whether the government had sold the certificate or not. This is simply one of those rare situations in which there are no losers and big winners.[1]

Tax lien certificates work like this:

Unpaid taxes become a lien on the property. This means that the tax obligation is recorded in the government's property records, and until the taxes are paid, the lien remains. If the taxes are not paid for a long enough period, the owner will lose the property. Meanwhile, a penalty of 8% to 50% per year is being added to the amount of the lien. Having a lien on the property means that nobody can buy the property without being subject to the lien. Government-issued tax liens are super safe; they're superior even to first mortgages.

To get their money quickly, many local governments sell their liens to private investors and issue certificates for the liens. Just as when the government owns the lien, a penalty is added to the lien while the taxes remain unpaid. Similarly, the property will be forfeited to the investor if the lien is not paid off.

By stepping into the shoes of the government, you obtain a right to get the government's interest and have the same rights over the property that the government would have.

## "TAX LIEN" STATES VERSUS "TAX AUCTION" STATES

The variety of state laws ensures that there is a state whose system fits your needs.

A comparison between California and Florida will help explain the difference between buying a tax lien and buying a property.

In California, if an owner does not pay the property taxes, the property becomes "tax defaulted," and the owner has five years to redeem the property. If the owner redeems, he must pay interest, penalties, and costs to the tax collector. If the owner does not redeem, the tax collector can sell the property.[2] The buyer at this sale will never be paid any interest. He is bidding on the property, and that is all he will get.

In Florida, by buying a tax lien certificate, you are purchasing the right to collect interest on the unpaid taxes. An auction is held at which the successful bidder is the person who agrees to accept the lowest rate of interest from the property owner. However, all tax lien certificates not sold at the auction can be bought from the county and will draw a full 18% interest without bidding. In Florida, you are not buying the property; you are buying the right to interest on the unpaid taxes. If the property owner still does not pay his taxes, then the property will be auctioned off. At this second sale, the bidders are after the property, not the interest.[3]

Each state can enact its own laws on subjects such as tax liens. As a result, there are many states where you can buy the right to interest on unpaid taxes, and yet, if the taxes and interest are still not paid, you can get the property without having to bid again or pay any more money. Getting property this way does not happen often, but it happens often enough to keep the process interesting. The variety of state laws ensures that there is a state whose system fits your needs.

In this book, I will focus on states where your investment will bring you a high rate of interest together with a high level of security. In these states, you can be delighted in the rare instances in which the taxes are not paid because you may then get the property for pennies on the dollar. I will tell you exactly how to do this.

First, however, I will explain in detail the mechanics of how tax lien certificates work and how to buy them. The point I want to make here is that this is not an exotic, concocted investment but a government-run program that serves the interests of the government as well as your interests. You can therefore rely on its legitimacy as you move on to learn its rules.

These ideas probably are new to you, so to get you primed for the adventure, in the next two chapters I will discuss what a world of difference the increased earnings of tax lien certificates will make to your investment program and how an investment in tax lien certificates compares to your present investments.

---

**Notes**

1.   Kotsopoulos, "Lien Sale Project Boosts City Coffers; Buyers Take Burden While City Gets Taxes," *Worcester Telegram & Gazette* (June 22, 2005).

2.   Cal. Rev. & Tax Code 126, 3691–92, 3707, 3426, 4101–2.

3.   A complete explanation of Florida's procedures is found in appendix II.

**CHAPTER 2**

# Why Would You Want a Tax Lien Certificate?

Tax lien certificates present you with an outstanding package of benefits.

## HIGH YIELD

The main attraction of tax lien certificates is their consistently high yield.

Exactly how high this yield is depends on where you invest. In Arizona, the top rate is 16%. Florida pays up to 18%. When tax lien certificates are bought at auction, your actual rate is determined by competitive bid. If this sounds confusing (and it should), I will explain the procedures of the various states in later chapters. If you cannot stand to wait, you can consult the comparative chart in appendix I.

The point here is that tax lien certificates should be prized as high-yield interest investments. At these rates of interest, this is more than just nice; it is a road to real wealth.

To get an idea of what a real difference those extra percentage points make, use the "Rule of 72." This is a quick way of telling how long it will take you to double your money. It works like this: Whatever your percentage of interest, divide it into 72. The answer will tell you how many years it will take your principal to double.

For example, if you are earning 5% at a bank, your money will double in just over 14 years. A corporate bond yielding 6% will double your money in 12 years. An 11% return in the stock market (the historical average) will double your money in just over 6 years and 6 months. By contrast, keeping your money in Florida tax liens at 18% will double your money in 4 years!

How important is the difference? Let's take a hypothetical investor who places $2,000 in a retirement plan at age 25. And let's be fair and assume that her investment averages 8% a year for the next 40 years. By the time she is 65, at this 8% rate, her money would have doubled more than four times. By contrast, had she invested in tax lien certificates earning 18%, her money would have doubled about 10 times. And how much would she have made? At 8%, our investor would now have around $43,000. At 18%, she would now, believe it or not, have more than $1,500,000. All from that one-time investment! Figure it out for yourself; our investor would retire as a millionaire from that one investment in high-yielding tax lien certificates.

## SAFETY

The second important trait of tax lien certificates is their safety. Tax lien certificates are secured by real property, which has been appraised by a government agency at an amount usually 10 to 100 times the amount of the lien.

Certainly, high interest rates are available in certain risky investments, such as junk bonds, but if those do not pay off, there is no security for the money to which you can turn.

## THE ABILITY TO START SMALL

The saying "It takes money to make money" is certainly true. However, it does not need to be true that it takes a lot of money to get a great return.

If you were buying a certificate of deposit, you might get a little more interest if you made a "jumbo" deposit of $50,000 or more. In tax lien certificates, by contrast, you can get the same high return regardless of the size of your investment. And because unpaid tax bills come in all sizes and you can buy just what you need, there will be an investment to suit your budget.

The saying "It takes money to make money" is certainly true. However, it does not need to be true that it takes a lot of money to get a great return.

In tax lien certificates . . . you can get the same high return regardless of the size of your investment.

## UNEXPECTED JOY

Although I emphasize the high interest rates provided by tax lien certificates, the possibility of obtaining property at unheard of bargain prices always exists, and many investors pursue tax lien certificates for just that purpose.

As I discuss in detail later, when you buy a tax lien in Arizona, for example, if you are not paid back your principal plus interest, three years later you can obtain the property, free of any mortgage. That's right! I am not talking about bidding for the property at a tax sale. There will be no other bidders. You will get a treasurer's deed from the county treasurer for just the cost of your tax liens.

This does not happen every day. But it does happen. And the thought that it could happen to you helps keep life interesting.

## TAX-DEDUCTIBLE TRAVEL

There is no rule
that auctions of
tax lien certificates
must be held at
dull locations.

There is no rule that auctions of tax lien certificates must be held at dull locations.

One of the most popular auctions of tax lien certificates is in Sedona, Arizona, in February. Sedona is a place where tourists flock all year to hike, go shopping for crafts, or visit the mysterious Seven Vortices. The mention of Telluride, Colorado, conjures up such vivid images of skiing and warming up in the lodge that nothing more need be said.

If you are going to these locations for investment purposes, the cost of your travel is added for tax purposes to the cost of the certificates you buy, and you will therefore pay less in taxes when you sell the certificates because you will have less of a profit. Furthermore, if you can make the case that you are in the business of buying tax lien certificates, your travel expenses are deductible immediately. As a rule, you cannot deduct travel to learn about or investigate investment opportunities.

## "BRAGGING RIGHTS"

Certainly, there are few topics more talked about than investments. Fred will talk about a hot stock that he bought on a hot tip just before it soared.

But Fred won't tell you about his investments that failed. And he won't make you confident that he can repeat his coup very often.

When you invest in tax lien certificates, you will have guaranteed yourself bragging rights. And your story need not be limited to the success you had last month but can include your system, which will reliably make you a winner next month—and every month. Your friends will know that this was not luck; they will think you are one smart person. And you are.

## CHAPTER 3

# How Do Tax Lien Certificates Fit into Your Investment Plans?

Tax lien certificates . . . are the best alternative for your investment plans.

Asked how he liked being 80 years old, Maurice Chevalier replied, "Considering the alternative, I like it fine." When it comes to investments, the only real answer to why you should put your money in tax lien certificates is that they are the best alternative for your investment plans.

That statement is especially meaningful because if there is one thing this world does not lack, it is investment choices: real estate investment trusts, January pork belly futures, oil drilling limited partnerships, callable convertible zero coupon debentures, and so on. We wander through a marketplace filled with sales agents grasping for any spare buck that manages to escape the tax man and the grocer.

One thing they all say is that you are a fool to put your money in anything as absurdly old-fashioned as a bank.

For example, you will be told that at 5% interest, you are losing money after taxes and inflation. But for the last eight years, Hogshead contracts have gone up at least 15 cents each May, and even if the price goes up only 10 cents this year, your $10,000 investment will grow to $17,000.

True enough, and if the price goes down only 10 cents, your hard-earned investment will shrink to $3,000.

If you had the mind of a medieval monk and the patience of a boulder, you could pore over endless charts and financial statements. But even though modern life is filled with competing demands, the usual methods of choosing investments—from guesswork, tips, and hope—will not do. If your choices are to reliably stand the test of time, you have some serious comparison shopping ahead of you. To talk meaningfully about the proper place of tax lien certificates then, we need to talk about the rest of the world. In this chapter, you will be pulled away from the noise and confusion of individual investment products so that you can take a moment to review and compare factors common to all investments.

Just as everything written in the English language is composed of just 26 letters and every color imaginable is composed of a mixture of only three primary colors, so, too, every possible investment product is composed of a mixture of a few primary traits.

Although to the sophisticated investor this discussion will sound old hat, remember that every great athlete spends the most time practicing fundamentals, not fancy strokes. You may be in more need of this break than a novice. Let us make a small side bet that after you read this chapter, you will find yourself thinking of your old investments in a new light.

## RISK–REWARD: TRITE AND TRUE

A college professor tells the story of a final examination he once supervised. While all the other students were hurriedly completing their tests, one student had not even begun to write. When asked what the problem was, the student said, "In preparing for this exam, I condensed the entire semester's work onto one page. I then condensed that page into one paragraph. Next, I condensed that paragraph into one sentence. Finally, I condensed that sentence into one word. But I forgot the word."

"That's baloney," the professor replied, disgusted. "That's the word!" rejoiced the student.

Just as the student in this story managed to abstract a subject until the result was meaningless, so the principle of risk–reward is too abstract a tool to result in a concrete plan of action. There is a fundamental wisdom in the principle of finding the right balance between risk and reward, but like most fundamental truths, it is so pervasive and condensed as to be overlooked or dismissed as commonplace.

Every abstraction works only by dropping off unique characteristics of the subject being abstracted. In investing, those unique characteristics distinguish success from failure. For our purposes, then, we are going to expand the number of categories under both risk and reward to include those that will be truly helpful in analyzing tax liens and other investments.

Just as everything written in the English language is composed of just 26 letters and every color imaginable is composed of a mixture of only three primary colors, so, too, every possible investment product is composed of a mixture of a few primary traits.

# REWARD FACTORS

Obviously, the essence of investing is the thought that placing what you currently have in a certain situation will cause you to have more later. For the purpose of comparing investments, you should consider exactly by what mechanism your profit is expected to be produced. In general, this will be through income potential or growth potential.

## Income Potential

The ability of an investment to earn you payments of money is its income potential. For example, if you put money in a bank, it will produce income in the form of interest. The money you put in the bank does not become more valuable (indeed, because of the effects of inflation, it becomes less valuable). But it earns more money and so has income potential.

Not too long ago, many people put their savings in mattresses or in boxes buried under trees. Leaving aside all other problems with these solutions, they clearly provided no income potential. If all went well, the money they took out would be the same money they put in—no more, no less.

Many investments are like money in a mattress, although this is not immediately obvious. If you buy a house to live in, although you hope that it will go up in value (a dim prospect in many areas at this time), it has no income potential unless you rent it out.

Similarly, gold bullion and diamonds are often bought as a hedge against inflation or social disruption. They may or may not serve these purposes, and they may or may not increase in value, but they have no income potential.

All other factors being equal, an investment with income potential is better than one without it.

The key phrase here is "all other factors being equal." They never are. A failing corporation may be paying dividends through selling off its assets, which, in turn, may diminish its prospects for future profits. No mechanical rule is a substitute for thought.

Just because an investment has income potential does not mean that its payments are regular or that you will be able to draw them out and live on them. It just means that the purpose of the investment is the production of payments.

Turning to tax liens, their obvious and superb strong point is

> Many investments are like money in a mattress, although this is not immediately obvious.

> All other factors being equal, an investment with income potential is better than one without it.

their income potential. In fact, I know of no other safe investment that pays such consistently high rates of interest.

## Growth Potential

The possibility that an item will increase in value is its growth potential. The hope here is that the item will decrease in supply or increase in demand so that its market value will go up. Every investment takes time. Income investments just ask you to wait for the future; growth investments require that you predict it.

Predicting the future is a risky business. Most people simply assume that whatever the trend is will continue. When a stock is rising, they assume that it will rise forever; when it is falling, they assume there is no floor. This is why most people sell investments when they are low and buy when they are high, which of course is exactly the opposite of what they should be doing.

One difficulty in foretelling the future is that it is influenced by more factors than can reasonably be considered. For example, real estate investors in southern California and New England took seriously Will Rogers's thought that real estate would continue to make money because no one was making any more of it. That takes care of the issue of supply. But when economic conditions that were not widely predicted caused those areas to be less desirable as places to locate, and when prices had risen so high that it was impossible to pay off a loan, the absence of demand caused prices to suffer greatly.

The second problem with making money by fortune-telling is that it is a competitive game. By the time you read a brilliant analysis of the future of a stock in a financial magazine, other investors who read it first, or who just had the same ideas, may have bid up the price of the stock, discounting in advance the predicted events.

As a general rule, competitive fortune-telling is a risky and unreliable way to make money.[1]

Tax lien certificates are not primarily growth investments. Their main attraction is their stunningly high interest rate.

Still, they are secured investments, and if the liens are not paid off, the property will be forfeited. This has occasionally resulted in spectacular growth opportunities for the holders of these certificates. Because their main purpose is income however, tax lien certificates will perform very nicely whether they produce a property windfall or not. This feature sets them above most growth investments.[2]

Income investments just ask you to wait for the future; growth investments require that you predict it.

As a general rule, competitive fortune-telling is a risky and unreliable way to make money.

# RISK FACTORS

## Market Risk

Market risk is the possibility that when you try to sell your investment, the market will value it less than you did when you bought it.

The most obvious example is buying a stock at its high point and later taking a loss when you sell after its value declines. All growth investments are subject to market risk, even those touted as immune.

For example, like most residents of Southern California, I was told that buying a home would be my best investment. It was pointed out that people in that area with the most modest incomes were rich in equity because bungalows they bought after World War II for $11,000 were being sold for $80,000. Everyone recommended that I borrow as much as I could get to buy the most expensive home possible. The idea was that values would rise faster than their interest payments, and I would pocket the difference. This is known as the principle of leverage.

For years this worked. I bought a house for $60,000 and sold it 12 years later for $150,000. Then I bought a house for $360,000 (borrowing even more money) and sold it only two years later for $550,000. The pace of this game was obviously quickening. I stretched and bought a house for $740,000.

Everyone was playing this game at the same time. It worked great! Until one day it didn't. I wrote the first edition of this book two years after buying that last house. It was on the market for $250,000 less than I paid. In a month, no one even came to look at it. Later, the house sold, and in a few years, its new owner was delighted as its value rose from the ashes, only to crash again in the current recession.

> Leverage is a powerful principle, but it works in both directions. It is a gun that sometimes fires backward.

Leverage is a powerful principle, but it works in both directions. It is a gun that sometimes fires backward. Today, hundreds of thousands of homeowners must, like me, repay their original purchase prices on homes that have gone down in value. There is no faster way to lose money. Market risk comes in several forms and may be caused by internal or external factors. Internal factors relate to how well the business is doing. If it is faltering, the business and any shares in the business may reflect this decline. As an example of an external factor, bonds may be bought for their income, but

How Do Tax Lien Certificates Fit into Your Investment Plans?

**17**

if they are sold before maturity, their value to other investors will depend on the interest rates that are available elsewhere. If interest rates have risen, the rate the bond will pay becomes less attractive, and so its value will be lowered to compensate.

This last example illustrates that market risk is most often a feature of growth investments rather than of income investments. If the bond is held to maturity as an income investment, market risk would not affect its value. Of course, bonds are subject to other risks, as discussed later in this chapter.

Tax lien certificates, like other income investments, carry no market risk. Delinquent property owners are compelled by law to pay high rates of interest; they have no real choice in the matter except to lose their properties.

As is discussed later, tax lien certificates have only limited liquidity. They therefore have no exposure, as do bonds on the secondary market, to fluctuating interest rates.

## Safety

The sales agents at Lincoln Savings had a powerful argument to customers cashing in their certificates of deposit: "What is the point in renewing your CD when you can get twice the interest in our bonds?" The only problem was that a bond is just a promise to pay, and this promise was not kept.

Obviously, the CDs that Lincoln's customers cashed were safer than the bonds because they were guaranteed by a federal insurance agency. But that agency itself had insufficient funds, and the only real safety lay in the hope that Congress would endlessly throw enough money at the agency to cover all its debts. Safety is a relative thing.

Concerning the safety of tax liens, most tax liens are paid off with interest. For example, Sean Coleman, treasurer for St. Joseph County in Indiana, told the *South Bend Tribune* that in 2007 the county collected $6.3 million in delinquent taxes, penalties, and fees.[3] More than $5 million of that money came from 1,582 payments made by taxpayers before the tax sale to ensure that their properties were removed from the tax sale list.[4] Still, we must remember that tax lien payers are a class of already delinquent people whose credit ratings we know nothing about. If you were to look at a tax lien certificate as a promissory note, it would be a miserable investment.

But tax lien certificates are more: They are a secured investment. If the landowner does not pay off the lien, you, as the holder of the tax lien certificate, can look to the property itself to pay off the lien. Because the amount of the tax lien is rarely more than a small percentage of the value of the property, this lien is completely secured.

By comparison, mortgage holders think that they are well secured if their loan is no more than 75% of the value of the property. They feel confident that the property will not drop by more than 25% of the appraised value until the loan is substantially paid down or paid off. A tax lien certificate rarely represents more than 5% of the property's value and is senior even to the first mortgage holder. The chance of a decline of more than 95% in the property's value from the county's appraisal is remote. This is obviously why these liens are almost always paid off. They are so thoroughly secured that only a rare property owner and his lender would both let the property be sold for this debt.

## Liquidity

The liquidity of an investment is your ability to sell it quickly and to convert it into cash.

The risk of loss of liquidity is twofold: First, there is the possibility that you will need the money invested so quickly that you will suffer a significant loss. This loss can come in the form of the familiar "substantial penalty for early withdrawal," which is imposed when funds in a CD are withdrawn before the certificate matures. It is also reflected in the "desperate owner" advertisements for home sales that are common today.

Second, in case the investment starts to slide in value, lack of liquidity will keep you on for a longer ride downward. Thus, when interest rates fell recently, those invested in money markets could shift their funds easily and without penalty. When home prices fell dramatically during the same period, sellers were unable to unload their houses quickly, if at all.

In the case of limited liquidity, higher reward tends to follow higher risk. Thus, financial institutions tend to pay higher interest rates on their longer-term CDs.

Liquidity is undeniably a weak point of tax lien certificates. Although in most cases the certificate can be assigned, and although a small secondary market is emerging, there is no mature secondary market for them as there is for stocks and bonds. Anyone investing in tax liens needs to assume the worst case: that the money will be unavailable until the debtor pays or the property can be sold.

Indeed, tax lien certificates have a form of unpredictable liquidity because the property owner can pay off the lien at any time. This feature is worse than callable bonds, for which the issuer is at least limited to certain time periods for redemptions. Still, bondholders typically redeem early because prevailing interest rates have gone down. The rate of return on tax lien certificates is set by law; as long as suitable certificates are available, the money can be quickly turned over to new certificates paying the same high rate.

## Overhead

Overhead is the expense of your operation. You cannot directly get it back, regardless of the success of the venture. For example, if a sales agent goes to visit a prospect, the cost of the gasoline he burns to get there is overhead. The sales agent hopes that the profit from the sale will justify the expense, but those funds are gone in any case.

In a sense, one cannot talk about overhead as a risk because those funds have been lost. Still, it is useful to think of overhead in this way, because the risk refers to the possibility that the eventual reward will not justify the cost to you.

Overhead need not necessarily be directly financial. Your labor has a market value, and spending it on one venture loses you the opportunity to spend it on another. If you spend your time canvassing a neighborhood as a door-to-door salesman, talking to brokers, or even researching investments, the time you spend is overhead.

The reason this risk is mentioned here is to distinguish investments that require personal time, effort, and money from those that don't.

Because there is only a small secondary market for tax lien certificates, locating and purchasing them takes a certain investment of time and money. At the far end of the scale, this may involve the time and costs of travel to the location of an auction. At the other end of the scale, it may involve Internet research or no more than the cost of a call to local officials to verify the existence of "leftover" certificates and the nature of the property.

Still, this amounts to more time and effort than that involved in calling a broker and ordering a stock or a bond. In those cases, the cash overhead is limited to the broker's commission, and the time overhead is limited to whatever research went into the selection.

The overhead in tax lien certificates may be deductible. The time investment in traveling, perhaps to resorts such as Telluride,

Colorado, and Miami, Florida, may be enjoyable, but in the current state of the market, tax lien certificates are a hand-picked investment.

# DEALING WITH RISK

There are several ways to respond to risk:

### Risk Avoidance

Your level of comfortable risk is determined in large part by your personality. However, appropriate risk depends as much or more on external factors.

The most primitive response to risk is complete avoidance. Because risk is a negative thing, this might at first seem to be the most sensible response. And it might sometimes be, if it were possible. For example, you might conclude that because all investments have risks, you should convert your savings into paper money and place the cash in a safe deposit box. You would then have successfully avoided investment risk. (Furthermore, this would be a great tax strategy, for without gain, there is no tax.) On the other hand, not only is this money earning nothing, but its value is also being steadily eroded by inflation, and so in place of risk, you get a certainty of loss. Low-earning, extremely conservative investments, such as insured bank CDs, most often ensure a loss because the rate of inflation plus the income taxes you must pay exceed your rate of return.

### Risk Management

The greatest protection against risk . . . lies not in the mechanical tricks of product diversification or dollar cost averaging but rather in sticking to quality.

The middle approach to risk is management. This involves determining and controlling the level of risk you are prepared to take and then locating the investments that will produce the greatest return for that level of risk.

Your level of comfortable risk is determined in large part by your personality. However, appropriate risk depends as much or more on external factors. For example, the level of risk that a young person can take is greater than that of a retiree because in a worst-case event, the young person may be able to earn the money back; the retiree cannot. Because the level of reward tends to follow the level of risk, young people are often counseled to follow their adventurous instincts in hope of larger gains. Other factors, such as job and marital status and amount of savings, must likewise influence sensible exposures to risk. For example, a young person with only a few dollars in savings is unwise to invest those scarce dollars in aggressive growth stocks, even if the risk is otherwise appropriate to his age.

Although you certainly need to figure out your level of comfortable risk and the chances of your investment getting you into trouble, you cannot just calculate the odds and see what happens; you need to reduce the likelihood of your nightmare coming true. You need to use risk management techniques.

The first technique of risk management is diversification. If you have studied computer stocks and believe that IBM, Apple, and Hewlett-Packard all have identical upside potential and identical risks, you should invest in all of them if your aim is to avoid large downside exposure. Even better diversification would be achieved by placing some of your funds outside the computer field altogether. Of course, logic will tell you that unless the risks are linked (for example, if you were insuring three packages on one ship against a disaster at sea), you are actually more likely to suffer some loss through diversification. Still, you are less likely to suffer a major loss.

Diversification need not be simply between products. One can diversify through time as well. Rather than fully investing all at once, if you spread your investments over time, you reduce the chances of having invested at a high point in the market and therefore suffering exposure to a down market. Of course, you reduce your chances of benefiting from having fully invested at the market's low point as well. As in the case of diversification between products, the theory of spreading investments over time is that the market as a whole will do well enough, and no one is wise or lucky enough to consistently time strategic moves.

The greatest protection against risk, however, lies not in the mechanical tricks of product diversification or dollar cost averaging but rather in sticking to quality. In any market, certain investments protect their owners better than others. Finding candidate investments, researching them before making a commitment, and knowing when to get rid of them, all require attention, courage, and often dull homework. Knowing the risks to which each investment is subject is the first step.

## Risk Exploitation

The highest level of response to risk is exploitation. For example, one of my clients buys polluted properties and cleans them up for residential development. The market hates these brownfields because their risks and the costs of cleanup are hard to predict. However, with expert investigation of the property, my client can take advantage of the market's aversion to the risks presented by these properties and buy them at a discount far deeper than would be offset by the cost of cleanup.

Risk exploitation is most successful when a single investor's close-up experience identifies situations that the market overlooked or reveals inaccuracies in the market's perceptions. Because the market is always on the lookout for opportunity, risk exploitation is often a creature of luck.

## PUTTING IT TOGETHER: THE PLACE OF TAX LIEN CERTIFICATES IN YOUR INVESTMENT STRATEGY

The typical investment advice you will hear is to divide your cash between money market funds, stocks, and bonds. The theory is that the money market funds provide liquidity, the bonds provide steady income and a hedge against interest rates falling, and the stocks provide an opportunity for growth. Through your life cycle, the proportion of these investments is supposed to change, with growth stocks being less represented as one ages.

In the current market, this strategy makes no sense. By most calculations, the stock market was, until recently, overbid and was sustaining its prices through application of the "greater fool theory." At present, the market's volatility makes any prudent calculation of value impossible. With interest rates the lowest that have been seen in years, bonds are in great danger because their value will fall as interest rates rise, and interest rates have nowhere else to go.

Tax lien certificates, on the other hand, are greatly outperforming the bond market and are doing far better than the long-term performance of the stock market, without its volatility. In this market, tax lien certificates can easily occupy the place in your portfolio that stocks, bonds, or both are usually recommended to fill. All that is lost in this transition is the liquidity of stocks and bonds. But stocks and bonds are not recommended for their liquidity. Rather, money market funds are typically used for their liquidity. Indeed, stocks and bonds have always been recommended as investments to be held at least as long as is typical for tax lien certificates.

> Tax lien certificates can easily occupy the place in your portfolio that stocks, bonds, or both are usually recommended to fill.

As with any other investment, how much liquidity you need depends on your financial and life situation. Clearly, unless you have a person ready, willing, and able to purchase your certificates from you at any time and at full value, placing all your spare cash in tax lien certificates would be a mistake.

On the other hand, with the interest rates on tax lien certificates as high as they are, and with historical returns on stocks being only 11% or so, tax lien certificates can easily occupy the place in your portfolio that growth investments, such as stocks, are usually recommended to fill.

As interest rates are hitting historic lows, many people on fixed incomes are taking maturing CDs and putting those funds into the stock market. This is almost certainly a mistake. Any investor who was in CDs in the first place was sufficiently concerned about safety that he or she can justify turning to the stock market in search of higher yields only by ignoring the risk.

One characteristic common to many people on fixed incomes is that they have leisure time; they are usually retired. The time overhead of tax lien certificates therefore does not lie as heavy on these investors as on those who must personally pursue other sources of income. For these investors, carefully chosen tax lien certificates are ideal.

Without a doubt, investing is an art. You need to find the right balance of risk and reward that satisfies your needs for liquidity, safety, and growth. This is a constant challenge as the market changes and as your needs change. If you work the unique and consistently profitable traits of tax lien certificates into your portfolio, you will have a top-flight investment plan for the 2010s and beyond.

---

## Notes

1.  For an introduction to the built-in psychological biases that lure us astray in our investment decisions, see Sewell, "Behavioural Finance" (May 2007) at http://www.behaviouralfinance.net/behavioural-finance.pdf. For a less technical and amusing treatment of this subject, see Blodget, "Born Suckers—The Greatest Wall Street Danger of All: You" (Dec. 14, 2004) at http://slate.msn.com/id/2110977.

2.  Chambers, "Tax Lien Process Hinders Progress," Herald-Dispatch.com (Oct. 4, 2007).

3.  Wensits, "Busy Time for County Treasurer," *South Bend Tribune,* News, p. B4 (Nov. 11, 2007).

4.  Ibid.

**$** = YES

BLANK = NO

| INVESTMENT | INCOME POTENTIAL | GROWTH POTENTIAL | AVOIDS MARKET RISK | SAFETY | LIQUIDITY |
|---|---|---|---|---|---|
| Tax Lien Certificates | $ | $ | $ | $ | |
| Residential Real Estate | | inconsistent | | $ | |
| Rental Real Estate | inconsistent | inconsistent | | $ | |
| Stocks | inconsistent | inconsistent | | inconsistent | $ |
| High Grade Bonds | $ | inconsistent | | $ | $ |
| Certificates of Deposit | $ | | $ | $ | |
| Money Market Funds | $ | | $ | $ | $ |

*Figure 1: Comparison of Sample Investments in the 1990s*

# How You Can Buy Tax Lien Certificates

**CHAPTER 4**

# Selecting an Area

Chinese sage Lao-tzu observed, "A journey of a thousand miles must begin with a single step."[1] The dividing line between successful people and dreamers is the taking of that first step. In this case, your first step is to decide, out of all the country's possibilities, what one state and what one county will be the target of your first purchase of tax lien certificates.

## NARROW THE AVAILABLE RANGE OF STATES

Your first stop will be appendix I of this book, which lists the available states that sell tax lien certificates. Look them over now.

The states that are not on this list sell delinquent properties at auction. You may find good bargains in properties at these sales, just as you will at all foreclosure sales. That is not what we are discussing here, however. Here, we are aiming primarily for a secured investment with a high interest rate.

## CONSIDER YOUR OWN STATE

Do you happen to live in one of the states listed in appendix I? If you do, this will be convenient because you may be more familiar with the neighborhoods in the county you pick, and if you decide to travel to that area, either to attend a tax lien auction (see chapter 6, "Bidding at Local Auctions") or to personally check out a property before you buy a lien from the tax collector (see chapter 8, "Armchair Values in 'Leftovers'"), you will not have far to go. Furthermore, as your collection of tax lien certificates grows, and as the time when you may be able to foreclose on one or more of these properties draws near, you may experience an intense curiosity to visit the neighborhood where you own tax liens.

For this reason, as you go through the additional considerations discussed in this chapter, if two states come close in your rankings, always give the nod to your home state.

As a second choice, give preference to a state in your region of the country. If you live in California, a state that does not sell tax lien certificates, you might therefore be partial to tax lien certificates issued by counties in Arizona.

## FOCUS ON YOUR OBJECTIVE: MONEY OR PROPERTY

Tax lien certificates are a unique investment in that they not only provide a high rate of secured interest, they also provide the opportunity to obtain real estate at fabulously low prices. Although I stress in this book the income potential of tax lien certificates, if you want to maximize the possibility of obtaining the property, you may be drawn to certain states.

The first factor you should look at if property is your goal is the general economic condition of the state. If a state is in a recession, with deeply depressed real estate prices and high unemployment, the chances that property will be forfeited are higher.

The second factor to consider is the laws of that state and whether they assist the owner of a tax lien certificate in obtaining the property.

For example, although Florida allows a very nice 18% on tax lien certificates, it gives a tax lien buyer no special edge in obtaining the property. As you will see in appendix II ("The 16% Winner's Circle"), in Florida, if your tax lien certificate is not redeemed, you can apply for a tax deed. The deed will actually go to the person who bids the most for the property. You are allowed to bid the amount you paid for your tax lien certificate, along with the interest you have earned and any cash you choose to add. But a complete stranger can show up and bid a higher amount in cash and take the property. Clearly, Florida is a state you go to for the interest rate.

By contrast, in Arizona, if the property owner does not redeem the tax lien certificate in three years, you can go to court and foreclose on the lien. After five years, you do not even need to go to

**If two states come close in your rankings, always give the nod to your home state.**

**The first factor you should look at if property is your goal is the general economic condition of the state.**

court; you can just go in to the county treasurer and apply for a deed. There is no auction. You do not need to outbid anyone. You do not need to dig into your pocket for more money than you have already paid. In Colorado, you can likewise just bring your tax lien certificate to the county treasurer after three years, and the treasurer will make out a deed. Arizona and Colorado make it easy to get the property.

Maryland is an extreme example of a state encouraging the transfer of the property. There, you must foreclose within two years, and for certain properties, you may foreclose only 60 days after obtaining your tax lien certificate.

## CONSIDER THE INTEREST RATES

I have put interest rates last among factors to consider in selecting a state precisely because most people put it first. Obviously, if all other factors were equal, you are better off getting 24% interest than you are getting 18% interest. But all other factors are never equal.

You also need to consider that if a state has a high interest rate, that may mean that the competition is stiffer in that state. For example, in early 1992, Iowa doubled its interest rate to a whopping 24%. Before then, competition for Iowa tax lien certificates was pretty low. After that increase, however, county treasurers have had no trouble selling the liens. The plan of visiting rural counties to buy tax liens at full rates is a great one but not if the deal is so overwhelming that others have beaten you there and there is little to choose from. You will always be better off with an actual 16% yield than a theoretical 24%.

Clearly, you should avoid states with low interest rates, but among states within a few points of each other, geography, economics, competition for the certificates, and other factors should be stressed.

## ZERO IN ON A COUNTY

There are more than 1,400 counties to choose from in 23 states and the District of Columbia. Although the rules for the sale of tax lien certificates are set by state law, the actual sales are made by local governments in each county. Even within a single state, the characteristics of counties vary dramatically.

Your first decision in selecting a county is to decide whether you want an urban or a rural area. I personally favor rural counties because the competition is often lighter and the staff has far more time and inclination to help me. Others prefer urban counties because there is a larger selection of properties or because they like the attractions of a particular city.

Again, you must ask whether you are looking for property or income. Counties vary in the percentage of properties that are redeemed.

## PINPOINT A NEIGHBORHOOD

In every county, there is a "good" area and an area "on the wrong side of the tracks." Certainly, you want your tax lien certificate to be on property in a desirable area.

There are several ways to check out areas within a county. A personal visit is a fine idea. Real estate brokers can help. However, one of the best sources is the staff of the local tax collector. (See chapter 10, "Getting Local Officials to Help You.") These officials can tell you not only which areas are nicest, but also which areas produce the highest rates of redemption.

---

**Note**

1.　Lao-tzu, *The Way of Life,* p. 64.

## CHAPTER 5

# What to Look for in Properties

*The only value of land lies in what you can do with it. The best proof that land can be developed is that it has already been developed.*

Now that you have focused on a state, a county, and an area, your next step is to decide what kinds of properties you want to consider.

A great variety of properties are available. They range from undeveloped land to land developed for residential, commercial, or industrial uses.

At first glance, it might seem as though the kind of property you get is not an important issue. All of these properties have been appraised as being worth much more than your tax lien certificate is going to cost. You might not mind getting any of these properties at such low prices. However, the kind of property you get can make a big difference.

Entrepreneur Dave Zussman says that research is the key to getting the best properties.[1] Zussman picks properties by examining data, including appraised values and geographic locations.[2] Zussman says that if you can't physically visit the properties, statistics can paint a detailed picture.[3] "What you don't want to do is buy a bunch of garbage," he says. "Just because it's a cheap lien does not mean it's a good lien."[4]

One tax lien investor was quoted in *Forbes:* "I was buying everything I could get my hands on, but I didn't realize how much junk I bought."[5] Because he had to foreclose on several properties that were difficult to sell, he figures that he's lucky if he's broken even. He concluded, "It's like walking through a mine field. You get blown up eventually."[6]

Although the article rightly concludes that care is necessary for this investment, there is hardly any investment where you will be safe buying everything you can get your hands on.

Surely you can take a wrong turn. For example, many parcels of raw land are sitting alone, out in the middle of the desert, with no access to water or utilities and perhaps with no roads in the area. These parcels may often be zoned as residential, but this has no practical meaning. In chapter 14 ("'Worthless' Properties") I go into more detail about the difficulties of an investment in raw land.

In an economic sense, the only value of land lies in what you can do with it. The best proof that land can be developed is that it has already been developed. No matter how high the appraisal on raw land may be, the pool of investors willing to check it out is small, and you could experience a long delay in selling it.

Industrial properties often need expensive cleanups. (See chapter 15, "Environmental Problems.") Both industrial and commercial properties are valued for the revenue they can produce and are therefore susceptible to economic downturns. Moreover, they tend to be expensive and therefore reduce the diversification that is important to any investment.

As you can probably tell by now, I am steering you toward residential properties. The reason for this is not that I am condemning investments in raw land or in commercial or industrial properties. On the contrary, vast fortunes have been made in such properties. My preference for residential properties lies rather in my focus on tax lien certificates as a secured, high-interest investment. Residential properties provide the benefits without the occasional complications.

This view of tax lien certificates as an income investment requires that as many of the properties be redeemed as possible. Certainly, the motivation of a property owner to redeem his home exceeds his motivation to redeem any other investment. Moreover, the problems, environmental and other, that might lead an owner to not want to redeem are far more rare in residential properties, as I discuss in detail in chapter 15.

However, all residential properties are not created equal. As I discuss in chapter 14, before you invest in a tax lien on a property, you need to have seen the assessment and how it is broken down between the land and the improvements. As a rule, the improvements should represent 75% of the total assessment. If they fall below 60%, either there is a lot of acreage, the land is fabulous, or the improvements are below par. You should skip such an investment. Often, the "improvement" on a property, when it represents a smaller fraction of the value, is a mobile home or a shack.

In checking out a property, there is always a dilemma between wanting the benefits of the investigation and hating the costs. If you were buying a property, it might be worthwhile to spend $3,500 on an environmental investigation and $500 for a property inspection. You might also want to see who the lenders are and whether any of them have been taken over by federal regulators. (See chapter 18, "FDIC Liens.") If all you are doing is investing $1,300 in a lien that has a 98% chance of being redeemed, it is impossible to justify much cost and effort.

Some properties are easy to check out. Others are not. A buyer could acquire a tax bill, see it go unpaid, claim the property, and then learn that below it are underground fuel storage tanks that must be removed and cleaned up at a cost of tens of thousands of dollars, according to Polk County Treasurer, Mary Maloney.[7]

"There's no such thing as a risk-free investment," Maloney says. "It's 'buyer beware,' because it's not my job to tell them what is or isn't a good investment. My job is to collect the taxes."[8]

In the end, the amount of effort and money you spend getting assurance that a property is a good place for your tax lien is a personal choice. My view, which I back up with my own money, is that the statistics of very high redemption rates, coupled with diversification and buffered by extraordinarily high returns, provide considerable comfort.

My advice to you is to augment that comfort by sticking to good neighborhoods, by investing only in improved properties, by limiting yourself to residential properties, and by checking the assessment to be sure that the improvement represents the lion's share of the value of the property.

At that point, if you cannot sleep easy, you probably weren't going to anyway.

This said, if you go to tax lien auctions, you will encounter people who bid on almost every property without knowing or caring much about any of them. How can this be? Often they are paying for these liens with large funds of pooled money. These investors are banking on the fact that most tax liens are paid off, and the few that are not can be investigated at leisure before foreclosure.

This statistical approach makes sense if you are bidding on scores of properties. But the statistical laws of large numbers do not apply if you are buying only a few liens, and you can improve your odds with a little focused investigation.

So, if you don't have the time, resources, or inclination to do the homework I suggest in this book, by all means consider becoming one of the customers of the person with bags of money, including yours, who bids on everything in sight. You will save yourself the research on individual properties, but your energies will merely be shifted to investigation of the bagholder and the fund.

---

**Notes**

1.  Murtaugh, Kirby, "Tax Lien Auctions: The Gain, The Pain," *Mobile Register,* A p. 1 (July 2, 2006).

2.  Ibid.

3.  Ibid.

4.  Ibid.

5.  Lubove, "Caveat Emptor," *Forbes,* p. 80 (Dec. 24, 1990).

6.  Ibid.

7.  Dobbs, "Bidders Jockey for Right to Pay Others' Tax Bills," *Des Moines Register,* Metro Iowa, p. 1B (June 21, 2005).

8.  Ibid.

Augment [your] comfort by sticking to good neighborhoods, by investing only in improved properties, by limiting yourself to residential properties, and by checking the assessment to be sure that the improvement represents the lion's share of the value of the property.

## CHAPTER 6

# Bidding at Local Auctions

The centerpiece of excitement and social life among those who invest in tax lien certificates is the annual auction. Note that I didn't say that the auction is the best way to buy tax lien certificates. My recommendations for getting the best bargains are in chapter 8 ("Armchair Values in 'Leftovers'") and chapter 9 ("Buying from Other Investors"). Still, you have not fully experienced the world of tax lien certificates until you have gone to the auction.

## WHEN IS THE AUCTION?

States that offer tax lien certificates generally hold an auction once each year. A few states allow counties to hold additional auctions of "leftovers," but these are rare. Exactly when the auction will be is outlined in state law but can often vary a little by county.

For example, in Arizona, each county holds its auction in February (which, incidentally, is a very nice month to visit Arizona). Colorado counties hold their auctions the second Monday in December (which, if you are a skier, is a very nice month to visit Colorado). I am sure you are seeing a pattern here and an extra reason to go to the auctions.

As soon as you have determined the state and the county you want to buy in, you should contact the local county tax collector, sometimes called the county treasurer, to find out the date, time, and place of the next auction.

# WHAT PROPERTIES ARE AVAILABLE?

While you are on the phone asking the treasurer about the auction, ask how you will be able to get a list of available properties. Each state's law requires the list of properties, along with at least some sort of description and the amount of taxes owed, to be published in the local newspaper. On the other hand, it is an awful bother to have to subscribe to the newspaper to get the list, and you would then end up knowing far more than you ever cared about the local doings in Hugmarump County.

The list is usually posted in the office of the tax collector, but that is probably not a convenient location for you.

In some counties you may purchase a computer-generated copy or compact disc or have an e-mail sent directly to you from the treasurer for a nominal fee. In Dawson County, Nebraska, for example, the fee is $15. In addition, in some counties, properties may be researched online.

Because bidding at auction may require your personal appearance—although many counties now hold their tax sales online—and because you need to spend some time checking out the properties anyway, you may not mind picking up a list when you get there.

# CHECKING OUT THE PROPERTIES

The process of locating the best residential areas where liens are available and determining which properties are adequately improved is described in chapter 10 ("Getting Local Officials to Help You"). Without repeating those instructions, I will add that if you are physically in the county, you should take advantage of that by visiting the neighborhoods and at least some of the properties that are on the list.

No matter how enthusiastic the other bidders are about a property at the auction, that does not mean they know anything about it. Don't follow a blind leader. Check out a property to your own satisfaction.

# CHECKING IN AT THE AUCTION

Some states have elaborate protocols for registering at the tax lien auction. For example, at the auction in Miami, Florida, you must register in advance and give the tax collector a form containing your Social Security number. You will then be given a buyer number. All bidders must then post an electronic deposit of 10% of their intended purchases, with a minimum deposit of $5,000 required through http://www.BidMiamiDade.com. You will be limited to purchasing no more than 10 times any deposit received by the tax collector. You will be allowed to increase your deposit by submitting an additional deposit authorization.

# HOW DO YOU BID?

The lowest bid is the winning bid. In effect, the auction is held as a sort of favor to the delinquent property owner.

In most states, the amount of money you are going to pay to get a tax lien certificate is exactly the amount of the delinquent taxes, plus the interest and penalties already owed to the county by the property owner. What you are bidding for is the amount of interest you are going to require the property owner pay to you.

Therefore, if the highest rate of interest allowed in that state is 18%, the first bid on the property is 18%. If another bidder wanted that tax lien, he would have to agree to accept less (e.g., 17.75% interest). The lowest bid is the winning bid. In effect, the auction is held as a sort of favor to the delinquent property owner. If the tax lien on his property is not sold at the auction, he will owe the maximum rate of interest.

Not all states work this way, however. In Colorado and Maryland, for example, the tax lien certificate goes to the person who pays the taxes, interest, and penalties owed, plus the largest amount of cash. The cash goes directly into the county's general fund. The property owner gets no benefit from the auction in these states, and the bidders can never be sure in advance how much money they will need to pay to get a certificate.

# WHEN DO YOU PAY?

Each of the states is very specific about when you owe the money and how you must pay it.

In Arizona, the entire amount of the bid must be paid via Automated Clearing House (ACH) debit on the Payments page of the Tax Sale Web site no later than 5 p.m. the day after the sale. Wyoming says that the county treasurer must be paid "immediately." There is no room for fudging here.

In Florida, by contrast, as soon as you are the lowest bidder, you must pay the tax collector a "reasonable deposit" within 24 hours. After your certificate has been prepared, if you do not pay the rest of the money within 48 hours, you lose your deposit.

Other places require payment by the next day or before the conclusion of the sale. If you fail to show up, the tax lien is merely auctioned off again.

# TACTICS AT THE AUCTION

There is really only one variable at the auction, and that is the intensity of the competition. And there is more competition than there used to be. In 2006 Adams, Arapahoe, Denver, and Jefferson counties in Colorado sold 51% more property tax liens to investors than in 2005: 10,398 versus 6,879.[1] The jump reflects several trends, including a sharp rise in mortgage foreclosures and homebuilders unable to generate the cash they need to cover taxes on their undeveloped lots.[2] Arapahoe County limited attendance at its November 2006 tax auction to 250, with 50 more people waiting to grab empty seats as people left, said Jan Neilson, deputy treasurer.[3] Almost 300 people registered to bid on more than 3,000 tax liens in Adams County in 2006, compared with 178 people in 2005.[4]

In the current economic climate, you will see more interest in tax lien auctions because of the low prevailing interest rates. At the same time, because of the continuing recession, there are plenty of tax lien certificates on the market.

It will be a pretty good year.

# CAN YOU DEDUCT THE TRIP TO THE AUCTION?

In general, no deduction is allowed for travel expenses for investigating new investments.[5] However, if you hold substantial investments in tax lien certificates, and you take a trip to buy more, an argument can be made that you are in the business of buying tax lien certificates, and therefore, your trip is deductible.[6] As a general rule, however, investors are not in a trade or business and cannot deduct expenses of obtaining investments as business expenses.[7]

Even if you are not in the business of buying tax lien certificates, however, your expenses related to buying the certificates are not lost forever. For tax purposes, expenses connected with acquiring an investment are added to the cost of the investment (in tax language, this total cost is the investment's basis).[8] When it is time to pay taxes, the higher your expenses, the lower your taxable gain. And even if you are not in the business of buying tax lien certificates, once you have the certificates, travel expenses spent looking after your investments (for example, arranging for foreclosure) will be deductible.[9] However, these deductions are among those that must exceed 2% of adjusted gross income before they do you any good. They are also subject to decrease for high-income taxpayers.[10]

---

**Notes**

1. Svaldi, "Lien Cuisine: Investors Are Gobbling Up Chances to Make Money at Auctions by Buying Liens on Overdue Property Taxes," *The Denver Post*, Business, p. C-01 (Nov. 17, 2006).
2. Ibid.
3. Ibid.
4. Ibid.
5. 1992 Prentice Hall Federal Tax Course, 2000(e), p. 2004.
6. Ibid.
7. Federal Tax Coordinator 2nd L-111 (1992).
8. Internal Revenue Code, 1012.
9. Federal Tax Coordinator 2nd. L-1400 et seq.
10. U.S. Master Tax Guide, 1012, 1013.

## CHAPTER 7

# Bidding Online

Recently some municipalities have instituted online tax sale auctions as an alternative to traditional tax sale auctions that require bidders to be present in person. Because these types of auctions are fairly new, you should familiarize yourself with the systems used in different municipalities.

Online tax sale auctions have the potential to make the process much more efficient and convenient. However, investors used to the traditional, in-person auctions will need to adjust to this new way of doing business.

Online auctions also increase the competition. Rather than just competing with people who go to the sale, you're competing with any bidder with a computer. So many more bidders participate. And because of the additional competition, lower interest rates may be bid for the certificates.

If you decide to participate in an online tax sale, make sure you still do your due diligence so you don't bid on liens on worthless or dangerous properties. (See chapters 15 and 16.) You should also know that you will pay more for tax lien certificates at an online auction than you will if you bid on them in person. That's because you will have to pay a commission to the online auction company. The commissions could be as much as 10% of the price you pay for the tax liens.

Municipalities that have instituted online tax sale auctions usually outsource their auctions. For example, various counties in Arizona, Colorado, and Florida have outsourced their tax sale auctions to Realauction.com.

Realauction.com tax sale auctions work like this: In the months before the opening of the auction, a custom Web site is created according to specifications set up by the county. Two months before bidding begins, a package is mailed to all previous and prospective bidders explaining the new sale procedures and providing the dates of scheduled training classes to be held at the county.

A demonstration site or trial auction is also opened so the bidders can test the system before the actual auction starts. Bidders may visit the site at any time to register to participate in the sale.

On the same day the county first advertises the property in the local newspaper, the list is published on the Web site. Bidders can enter their bids anytime before the auction ends.

In order to be eligible to win tax lien certificates (not just bid), participants must meet the county's deposit requirements. Bidders are encouraged to use the Automated Clearing House (ACH) wizard on the Web site. Deposits can also be made using cash, wire transfers, or counter checks.

In order to make the sale easier to manage for bidders, certificates are individually placed on sale in groups called batches. The county decides the size of the batches, but generally, they are blocks of 500 or 1,000 certificates each. The county decides the day when the auction officially ends. At a specific time on that day, the first batch officially closes, and the winners are determined.

The results are posted within five minutes after a batch closes. The batch format allows bidders to see the auction results and decide whether they need to adjust their future bids. Bidders can also make additional deposits at any time during the sale. After all batches have closed, bidders can pay for their certificates through the ACH wizard on the site. The unofficial results are posted on the site along with other statistics regarding bidding patterns.

In addition to ACH transfers, Realauction.com allows the county to accept additional methods of payment, including wire transfers, cash, and counter checks.

Likewise, with the click of a computer mouse, investors can bid on tax certificates in Florida's Palm Beach County, which started selling tax certificates online in 2005. Holding the auctions online eliminates the confusion that ensued during live auctions, says Paschal Poston, director of tax services for the tax collector's office.[1]

During live auctions, large numbers of bidders bid for the same certificate, making it difficult to determine who bid first, Poston says. The online auction eliminates any confusion, he says.[2]

The following is a snapshot list of county auctions handled by Realauction.com:

ARIZONA:

Arizona online auctions open in January and end in February.

PRACTICE WEB SITE, ARIZONA COUNTIES: http://www.
arizonataxsale.com/

COCONINO COUNTY: http://www.coconinotaxsale.com/

YAVAPAI COUNTY: http://www.yavapaitaxsale.com/

COLORADO:

Colorado online auction Web sites open in October, and the
auctions end in November.

PRACTICE WEB SITE, COLORADO COUNTIES: http://www.
coloradotaxsale.com/

ADAMS COUNTY: http://www.adamstaxsale.com

ARAPAHOE COUNTY: http://www.arapahoetaxsale.com

DENVER CITY & COUNTY: http://www.denvertaxsale.com

WELD COUNTY: http://www.weldtaxsale.com

FLORIDA:

Florida online auctions open in May and end as late as June 1.

PRACTICE WEB SITE, FLORIDA COUNTIES: http://www.
floridataxsale.com/

COLUMBIA COUNTY: http://www.columbiataxsale.com/

HERNANDO COUNTY: http://www.hernandotaxsale.com/

HILLSBOROUGH COUNTY: http://www.hillsboroughtaxsale.com/

LEE COUNTY: http://www.leetaxsale.com/

LEVY COUNTY: http://www.levytaxsale.com/

MONROE COUNTY: http://www.monroetaxsale.com/

PINELLAS COUNTY: http://www.pinellastaxsale.com/

POLK COUNTY: http://www.polktaxsale.com/

PUTNAM COUNTY: http://www.putnamtaxsale.com/

SEMINOLE COUNTY: http://www.seminoletaxsale.com/

SUWANNEE COUNTY: http://www.suwanneetaxsale.com/

More than 50 counties have outsourced their online tax sale
auctions to Bid4Assets.com. These include the following Florida
counties: Alachua, Brevard, Charlotte, Duval, Escambia, Gadsden,
Gilchrist, Santa Rosa, Sarasota, Taylor, and Walton. In these counties,
three to four weeks before a tax sale auction, Bid4Assets.com
posts a complete list of the available properties. If bidders have any
questions after reviewing the information included in the auction

listing, they are encouraged to contact the tax collector's office of the county in which the property they are interested in is located.

Most counties require bidders to place a deposit before they make their first bids. Deadlines to place these deposits are set for seven days before the close of the last auction for a particular county. The acceptable deposit methods vary from county to county.

When bidders are ready to place a bid, they choose a bid type, enter their bid amount in the "Bid Amount" box, and click on the "Bid on This Item" button. Before bidders can place a bid, they will be prompted to log in or register if they haven't already. Once bidders have submitted their bids, Bid4Assets.com will send them a bid confirmation notice via e-mail and place a similar notice in their "My Messages" inboxes.

The winning bidder will receive an e-mail (and message in his inbox) from Bid4Assets.com with settlement and deed transfer instructions within 24 hours. If you are the winning bidder, your deposit will be transferred to the county tax collector as a nonrefundable down payment for the property. If you are not the winning bidder on the auction, your deposit will automatically be refunded within 10 business days of the close of the auction.

As in every field of commerce, online access to tax lien auctions is taking hold and changing at a dizzying pace. You should consult the Web page of the specific locations in which you are interested, and then, check back often to be sure nothing has changed.

Finally, do not allow mechanization to distract you from the fundamental principles of the investment that I outline here. Just as the appearance of online stock trading did not make fundamental research obsolete, a lessening of the physical effort of buying tax lien certificates should not lessen the intelligence and diligence you apply to investigating the properties.

---

**Notes**

1.   Sorentrue, "County Tax Sales, Going, Going, Gone over the Internet," *Palm Beach Post,* Local, P. 1C (June 2, 2006).

2.   Ibid.

## CHAPTER 8

# Armchair Values in "Leftovers"

## WHY BUY DIRECT FROM THE TAX COLLECTOR?

As you will discover when you attend your first tax lien auction, they are interesting, exciting, and profitable. You will make new friends and pick up tips from pros. But remember, the whole point of an auction is to place you in competition with others in order to reduce your profit. But what if there were a way you could bypass this process and get the maximum interest that the state allows? You can.

The whole point of an auction is to place you in competition with others in order to reduce your profit.

The fact is, there are billions of dollars in available tax liens spread over more than 1,400 counties in 23 states and the District of Columbia. There have always been more tax liens than demand from tax lien investors. Not at every time and at every place, but always and in many places.

Several states have laws that specifically provide that if a tax lien does not sell at the auction, you can then go directly to the county tax collector and buy it. You do not need to bid against anybody. The interest rate will be the highest possible. You do not even have to physically go to the tax collector's office. This is as close to ideal as investing gets.

In some states, the rush for unsold certificates can be greater than at the auctions. Of course, you must check to be sure that the county you pick has leftover liens and, indeed, that the state you pick allows direct purchases after the auction. Some states, such as Iowa, provide that if any leftovers exist, they will be auctioned off at another time.

## TIPS ON BUYING DIRECT

### Try Smaller Counties

The major drawback in buying directly from the tax collector is that you may buy only what was not bought by anyone else at the auction. This certainly means that the selection is less, and it could mean that there are no available properties at all in that county, or at least none that you want.

Your chances of finding good direct buys are greater in more rural counties where the auctions draw far fewer people.

### Buy Early in the Year

Whenever you buy a tax lien certificate, you must pay the treasurer not only the back taxes, but also whatever interest and penalties have accrued up to that time.

There is no real disadvantage in this as long as the tax lien certificate is actually redeemed. In fact, you will be earning interest on this larger amount of money. But if the property is not redeemed, and if you can eventually turn in the tax lien certificates and be handed a deed for the property, any extra amount you pay for the certificate comes out of your own pocket because you could have gotten the same property for less.

### Establish a Relationship with Local Officials

The system I prefer for buying tax lien certificates depends on relationships with county employees working in places that are not always easy to get to. Most businesses depend, at their root, on personal relationships, and this one is no exception. In chapter 10 ("Getting Local Officials to Help You"), I explain my system in detail.

## CHAPTER 9

# Buying from Other Investors

## BARGAINS IN TAX LIEN CERTIFICATES FROM OTHER INVESTORS

By now you know that tax lien certificates are a spectacular investment. But what if you could buy them at a discount?

You will recall that in chapter 3 ("How Do Tax Lien Certificates Fit into Your Investment Plans?"), I discussed a negative point about tax lien certificates—their low liquidity. Because there is no organized private market for buying or selling tax lien certificates, it is possible that some investors who had not expected to need the money before cashing in their certificates now feel differently. Finding a distress sale, whether through word of mouth or through advertisements, may be more of an effort than simply buying a certificate from a county, but it may be worth it.

Just remember, regardless of the source of your certificates, whether from the county governments or private investors, you need to check out the properties before you buy them, as I explained in chapter 4 ("Selecting an Area") and chapter 5 ("What to Look for in Properties").

## MANAGING LIQUIDITY THROUGH RELATIONSHIPS

The search for a bargain is not the only reason you might be interested in the transfer of tax lien certificates. You might decide to join with one or more investors and buy tax lien certificates in the same area, with an understanding that if one of you needs to cash out, the others will pick up the certificate.

By now you know that tax lien certificates are a spectacular investment. But what if you could buy them at a discount?

Finding a distress sale, whether through word of mouth or through advertisements, may be more of an effort than simply buying a certificate from a county, but it may be worth it.

Such an arrangement not only provides extra liquidity, but it also can make for some good vacations as you travel to your favorite tax lien–selling resort with your friends.

## HOW TO TRANSFER TAX LIEN CERTIFICATES

States that sell tax lien certificates have provisions specifically allowing you to assign a certificate to another person. After all, an assignment is how you got your lien from the county in the first place.

Just because you fill out this form does not mean that the certificate is transferred. At this point, the county would know nothing about the sale. If the tax lien certificate is redeemed, the county would assume that the person who bought it still owns it, and it would pay the redemption money to that person.

For this reason, it is of vital importance to register the transfer of the tax lien certificate with the county. This usually requires that the tax lien certificate be sent to the county and may require a nominal fee, such as $2.25 in Florida.

## CHAPTER 10

# Getting Local
# Officials to Help You

## BREAKING THE GIBBERISH BARRIER

Having read chapters 4 and 5, suppose you have decided what states you want to consider for your tax lien investments, and you know what kinds of properties you want to target. Three years ago, you made the trip to Arrowhead County for the tax auction, but right now you are looking for some of those "Armchair Values in 'Leftovers'" I described in chapter 8.

You consult the Web page or pull out your copy of the local newspaper that listed the properties that were available for this year's auction. The list is not too informative. It begins:

| PARCEL NO. | OWNER | DLQ TAX |
|---|---|---|
| 145-02-00700 | Lefoe, Manny & Freda | 427.06 |
| 145-02-00975 | DuPres, Charles Q. | 381.12 |
| 145-02-01765 | B & Q Builders | 967.53 |
| 145-03-00276 | Futheng, Hans & Bertha | 476.98 |
| 145-04-01987 | FBN PRESS | 1,254 |
| 146-01-00145 | Bigelot, Norma | 767.50 |
| 146-01-00568 | Lupis, Jan and LeRoy | 2,187.75 |
| 146-02-00986 | Second Story Title | 1,347.32 |

Obviously, you have no idea what these parcels look like, where they are, or what is on them. Any of them could already have been sold at the auction, and some could have been bought just afterward for the full interest rate. It's time to call in Ethyl.

No, I don't mean that you need a higher grade of gasoline. I mean Ethyl, the deputy county clerk. And really, I don't mean my Ethyl. She's my secret.

You need to find your own Ethyl. I will tell you how.

You e-mail the list to Ethyl with a note asking her which parcels are still available. She sends your list back. Ethyl has noted 15 of the properties. Time for a call to Frank at the county assessor's office.

What you need from Frank is a breakdown of the assessments to show how much is allocated to the land and how much to the improvements on these properties. If the land's assessed value is more than 40% of the total assessment of the property, you should skip this property. In a couple of minutes, you have 11 good properties.

Now, here is where Ethyl really helps beyond any call of duty. You don't know where these properties are, and for that matter, you know nothing about the county in which you are buying. Ethyl does. First, though, you need to take the time to chat with her. After all, she lives in a small town, working in an office where there is plenty of time to chat. She asks about your boy, John, who just applied to college and tells you about her niece's wedding last weekend. It seems hard to believe that you met Ethyl only one time.

You turn the conversation around to neighborhoods. Ethyl mentions the tax lien certificates on Wintergreen Heights. She says that this is a resort area where there are many second homes. It's at least as nice as Copper Corners, where you have been buying. "In fact," she says, "just about everything in Book 146 is good."

After a little while, you tell her which five properties you want. The last thing you need to know is exactly how much the interest and penalties have added up to on these properties since the time of the auction. She tells you, and you reply that you'll get a check out to her today. You talk a little longer, and you tell her you'll call in a few weeks.

Today is the 15th of the month. If you get your check out today, she'll be sure you get the interest for a full month (that's an extra $150 for every $10,000 you're investing at 18%). If you didn't know Ethyl, the clerk might not allow your interest to start running until the month after your check cleared or wouldn't accept your personal check at all.

# FINDING YOUR OWN ETHYL

Sound too good to be true? In many places, it is. In Dade County, Florida, for example, the clerks are so busy that the local rules require you to figure out for yourself how much money is owed on a property, where it is, and what is on it.

The answer is simple: Focus on the less-populated rural counties. In many of these places, life is slow, and your Ethyl has the time and the inclination to be neighborly. Besides, in a small town, your Ethyl will know every neighborhood, if not every block, and will be pleased to share what she knows.

Another advantage of shopping for tax lien certificates in a rural county is that there is much less competition. Although scores of people may show up for a tax lien auction in Denver or Orlando, greater bargains may be available in a smaller city with no bidding down from the maximum rates of interest. As I mentioned before, increasingly, groups of investors are pooling their money to compete for the tax lien certificates.[1] In fact, in a tax sale auction in Baltimore in 2006, three groups of investors paid a total of more than $8 million to buy up nearly three-quarters of the liens.[2] These investors "have the capital to invest in dozens if not hundreds of properties," says Michael Sanderson, legislative director for the Maryland Association of Counties. "These are sophisticated investors."[3] You are less likely to have to compete against them in a rural county. To establish the kind of relationship I am describing, it is likely that you will have to limit the number of counties in which you are investing. This is certainly no hardship. In my experience, even the smallest county will have more qualifying properties ready for your investment than you are likely to need.

If possible, begin your relationship in person. This is not to say that you cannot establish fast friendships entirely by phone. Still, these things are much better done in person. Besides, the better you know an area, the more comfortable you will feel with your investments, and the more enthusiastic you are likely to be about the possibility of obtaining property in the area at a bargain price.

If you do call, keep in mind that the person who handles tax lien sales might go by different names in different states. In some states, the county auditor handles the sales; in others, the treasurer does this; in still others, you must ask for the tax collector. (For the prime states detailed in appendix II, I tell you which office to contact.) You

> To establish the kind of relationship I am describing, it is likely that you will have to limit the number of counties in which you are investing.

should also know that not all states refer to the sales as tax lien sales. In Mississippi, for example, the sale is called a land tax sale.

When you find your Ethyl, no matter how helpful she is, you must not become a pest. When you call, you should be very specific about what you are looking for, and you should have done your homework by reviewing all the information you have available, including the procedures used by the state, as described in appendix II.

There is some basic political etiquette you have to respect. Ethyl is not going to be too popular with at least one property owner in her county if she helps you into a position where you can foreclose on property. Particularly if you are not a resident in her county, you can't help her boss get reelected or reappointed. She will not mind assisting you in finding and paying for tax lien certificates because the local voter would have been liable for the same interest and penalties anyway. Still, mentioning foreclosure is about as welcome as mentioning malpractice to a doctor.

You can ask her which areas have the highest redemption rates and which have the lowest. Nevertheless, when you casually chat, you must be a person after a high rate of return. And as a practical matter, that's what you are.

Nothing can take the place of personally inspecting each property. Still, having Ethyl's help comes mighty close.

> Ethyl is not going to be too popular with at least one property owner in her county if she helps you into a position where you can foreclose on property.
>
> Nothing can take the place of personally inspecting each property. Still, having Ethyl's help comes mighty close.

---

### Notes

1.  Schulte, Arney, "Housing Boom Boosts Liens' Appeal; Tax Sales That Once Drew Mild Interest Now Attract Deep-Pocketed Investors," *The Baltimore Sun,* Telegraph, p. 13A (March 25, 2007).

2.  Ibid.

3.  Ibid.

# How to Get Your Money or the Property

**CHAPTER 11**

# How to Redeem Your Certificates

Not much needs to be said on the subject of redeeming tax lien certificates because one of their nicest features is that the work of processing a redemption is done for you by the local treasurer.

If the property owner decides to pay off the lien, he does not contact you. Rather, he goes to the treasurer's office and pays the delinquent taxes, penalties, and interest. In some states, he gets a certificate of redemption in return for this, which he can record. In most places, he just gets a receipt.

Next, the treasurer goes to the records to see who gets the money. In places where you will keep the original tax lien certificate, a notice will go out to you that the property has been redeemed and that you should send in the certificate. After the treasurer receives the certificate, he mails you a check. In places where the treasurer keeps the original certificate on file, he just mails you the check. You should be aware that some time could pass if the treasurer's office is busy. You will be earning no interest at all during this period.

In a few states, such as Georgia, you will also need to sign a quitclaim deed, in which you acknowledge that you have no further interest in the property.

In order to fully appreciate the ease and comfort of this arrangement, you need to have invested in, for example, second trust deeds. There, not only do you have to worry whether you are adequately secured, but you have to establish a relationship with the debtor, check his credit, take his payments, and listen to his sad stories. With tax liens, the treasurer provides all these services for free. Best of all, unlike second trust deeds, you do not even care whether you are paid off, because you would be more than happy to get the property free of senior mortgages in return for the few cents on the dollar you have invested. In the case of a second trust deed, you would still have to pay off the senior lender, which could cost you thousands or even hundreds of thousands of dollars.

At this point, I must remind you that when you change your address, you must go through your tax lien certificates and put the treasurers on your list of people to notify. Unless there is a local form, the best way to do this is in a letter that lists the parcel numbers and your certificate numbers and requests that the records be changed to reflect your new address. Any other owners of your certificate should also sign the letter.

It is not at all unusual for property owners to wait two years or longer before redeeming the property. By that time, if you have moved, the Post Office may have stopped forwarding your mail, and you would have no way of knowing of the redemption. The amount of interest lost in this transition can be large because once the property is redeemed, no one is paying you interest on your certificate. Even worse, if you fail to claim the money in a reasonable time, which is sometimes fixed by statute, you may lose your rights to it.

One of life's best financial events is getting a check in the mail much larger than the one you wrote to get your tax lien certificate. And you know that getting this check is not largely the result of luck, as it so often is with the stock market, but is something you can reliably do again and again.

Take a moment to congratulate yourself. But do not rest on your laurels. Remember, this check means that you are no longer earning that high interest rate on these funds. The figures I gave you showing that you can earn more than $1 million on a single $2,000 deposit requires that you keep that money hard at work for you. If you let it snooze in a money market account until you can recycle it into another tax lien certificate, your returns will be dramatically less.

One of life's best financial events is getting a check in the mail much larger than the one you wrote to get your tax lien certificate.

## CHAPTER 12

# Foreclosing on Tax Liens

*The sun is just sinking behind the New York skyline, and lights are appearing all over the city and on the boats cruising the river. No matter how often Jim sees this from his New Jersey riverside condo, he thinks it is the best show in town. And his next thought is that if his condo wasn't the best buy in town, he doesn't know what was. Just $10,000 in tax lien certificates got him this $200,000 place! And his other tax lien certificates have bought him the time to retire and enjoy it. Not bad for 49 years old. Life is just beginning again.*

As though the super-high interest rate of tax lien certificates were not enough, they sometimes bring an extraordinary bonus. That a foreclosure on a tax lien does not happen every day will increase the thrill when it does happen.

The first thing to understand about tax lien foreclosures is that every state has its own requirements. Some states require you to post a notice of the foreclosure in three public places; others require none. Some states require you to run advertisements for four weeks, some for two, and some for none. Even if you know the procedure perfectly in one state, it will mean nothing in another.

The second thing to understand about tax lien foreclosures is that the law is strict about procedures. Any failure to follow the required process may stop you from getting a deed to the property or may make any deed you do get void. This is a time to be precise.

It is also, in my opinion, a time to get a lawyer. I say this with some bias because I am a lawyer. But there is a lot at stake here, and the costs of a lawyer are easily justified. If you get the property, you'll be getting it for pennies on the dollar. And if the debtor pays up during the process, he will often have to pay your attorney's fees. Besides, in most states you are going to have to go to court, where you will have to file pleadings and present evidence. Any mistakes may result in your case being thrown out. The judge, who does not know you, is unlikely to cut you any slack. This is no time to be cheap. When I am in this kind of situation, I hire local counsel.

In appendix II, I review the foreclosure requirements in several states. In this chapter, I will review the features that are common to all states.

## NOTICE OF FORECLOSURE

All states require that before you foreclose on property, you must give notice to those interested in the property.[1] This is a requirement not only of state law but also of due process under the U.S. Constitution.[2] The statutes nonetheless vary in their details concerning what the notice must contain, who gets notified, and how.

The person who is listed on the property records as the owner of the property must receive notice of the foreclosure. Often, the law will require that people actually on the property must be notified, too.[3] This is sensible and fair, as those people could hold a long-term lease that is about to be wiped out. Furthermore, mortgage holders must be notified.[4] Courts have held that among the parties entitled to notice are heirs of the property owner and other parties holding tax lien certificates.[5] This last notification is not strictly relevant as to holders of other tax liens because in many states, you are required to pay off these lienholders before foreclosing. Even were you not so required, you must, as a practical matter, pay off other tax liens, or the holders of these liens could simply foreclose on your title.[6] The notice to mortgage holders will often trigger them to pay off your lien because if the foreclosure goes through, their mortgage will be wiped out.

If the property owner is known and can be located, "personal service" is most often required. This involves hiring a process server to personally deliver the notice. Each statute will specify when service by certified or registered mail should or must be made.

All states allow "service by publication," that is, notification in a specified newspaper, to substitute for personal service if the person to be served cannot be located.[7] Although absolutely no one looks through the legal notices to see whether maybe some item applies to him, the law pretends that everyone does. Often, the state law requires publication in a newspaper, even if you have personal service, just in case some unknown person has an interest in the property.

You cannot get too cute about notification. In one case, a lien-holder gave notice in the English language in a newspaper printed in a foreign language, apparently thinking that the owner would surely not be browsing through that newspaper. The court threw the notification out.[8]

The courts can get extremely technical even when no tricks are being played. One line of cases in Missouri holds that the use of initials in the notice is invalid where the property owner uses his or her full name on the deed.[9]

Some states require posting on the property or public places as part of the notice procedure. The notice must adequately describe the property to be foreclosed. If it does not, the notice is no good, and the court lacks jurisdiction.[10] This means that the property owner or the mortgage holder can attack your deed even if they do not appear at the foreclosure proceedings. In addition, the notice must say when and where the proceedings are to be held, the name of the owner of the land, and the kind of taxes due.[11]

If notice is not properly given to some person, but he shows up at the proceedings anyway, the failure to give good notice is waived.[12]

## DO YOU HAVE TO GO TO COURT?

### What Happens in Court?

What the judge is interested in is whether your papers are in proper form and whether they recite all the facts required for you to be entitled to foreclose, including the required notification of the proceedings.[13]

Sometimes the property owner will come in and argue that the foreclosure should not take place. Occasionally, he is right, such as when he can prove that he really paid the taxes but did not get proper credit. A claim that the property was assessed too high comes too late, however, unless he can prove that this was some sort of fraudulent scheme to make him lose his property. Most of the time, though, the proceedings are default, meaning that no person opposing the foreclosure appears.

## What Do You Get from the Court?

The results of the court proceedings differ from state to state. In most states, the tax collector or some other official is ordered to issue a deed.[14] In Florida, all you get is an order that the property be sold to the highest bidder, and you are allowed to bid in the value of your tax lien certificate, plus the interest you have earned.

# WHAT ABOUT TAXES?

Odd as it may seem, there is no regulation clearly covering whether foreclosing on a tax lien and getting the property is a taxable event. If it is, you will owe income tax on the difference between the value of the property and the cost of the tax lien. If not, you will pay tax on your gain when you sell the property.

At this point, you should protest that all you did was get some property at a bargain price. If I sell you my new $20,000 car for $1,000, you do not owe income tax on your $19,000 "gain." A tax will be owed only if you sell the car for more than you paid.

However, the IRS has a regulation that says that if "mortgaged or pledged" property is "bought in" by the creditor for less than the value of the property, then gain is realized in the amount of "the difference between the amount of those obligations of the debtor which are applied to the purchase or bid price of the property . . . and the fair market value of the property."[15] The idea behind this regulation is that because the creditor will be able to deduct a bad debt if the property is sold for less than the mortgage,[16] he or she should be required to declare a gain if the property brings the creditor more than the mortgage.

Of course, in the case of tax lien certificates, we are not talking about "mortgaged or pledged property." Nevertheless, you may need to argue about whether you owe the tax upon foreclosure or upon sale of your new property.

If you are worried about this somewhat remote possibility, managing it should not be too much of a problem. First, you can control when the foreclosure occurs. You would plan on foreclosing early in the year so that you have time to sell the property before the end of the year. That way, if you do owe a tax, you will have the money to pay it. Second, you would market the property right away. Having bought it cheap, you can afford to offer someone else a bargain for a quick sale. You should take these actions regardless of tax issues in order to keep your funds earning at tax lien rates.

No question, taxes are annoying, and uncertainty in taxes is doubly annoying. Still, it is better to have gained and been taxed than never to have gained at all.

---

### Notes

1.  85 Corpus Juris Secundum, Taxation, 740.
2.  72 American Jurisprudence 2d, State and Local Taxation, 916.
3.  Ibid., 914.
4.  Ibid., 897.
5.  Ibid.
6.  Ibid., 965.
7.  Ibid., 928.
8.  Ibid., 916.
9.  Ibid., 922.
10. Ibid., 915, 919.
11. Ibid., 918.
12. Corpus Juris Secundum, 740.
13. American Jurisprudence 2d, 741.
14. Ibid., 973.
15. IRS Regulation 1.66-6(b).
16. IRS Regulation 1.66-6(a).

## CHAPTER 13

# Managing and Marketing Foreclosed Properties

Congratulations! You hit a home run in the tax lien game and landed what may be the best bargain of your life! You have a property that is worth 10 to 50 times what you paid for it. Go ahead and cheer; go out and celebrate. You are, quite rightly, thrilled.

What should you do next? For example, if you get a property in your favorite beach or mountain resort, if you're like me, you'll keep it. For most of us, though, our investment cycle is not complete until we translate our new property into cash.

Selling a property you acquired through foreclosure of a tax lien is similar to selling property you acquired any other way. However, there are some special factors to consider and some points worth stressing.

## GET LIABILITY INSURANCE

As a very first step, call an insurance agent in the area of your new property and get liability insurance. You are now the owner of the property, and people will be coming through it. You have no real idea what condition it's in. Protect yourself. And while you're at it, get fire insurance too. You have no lender to remind you and to require this. However, you now have an investment to protect.

## CONSIDER A QUIET TITLE ACTION

Second, even though you have the title, you should consider bringing a quiet title action. This is a lawsuit brought against any potential claimants to the property in which you seek a declaration from the court that you hold good title. This court judgment will help protect you against any later legal challenges to your title by people who think that they were not given the required notice, that the description of the property was not adequate, and so on. The person who buys the property from you is going to want to be assured that she is getting good title. She is not trying to buy a lawsuit with the former owner. Likewise, a title insurance company may require you to do this.

## BRING ANY NECESSARY UNLAWFUL DETAINER ACTION

Just because you now have legal title to the property does not necessarily mean that the former owners or any tenants, guests, or squatters have left or have any desire to leave. As the new owner, you could be in a position similar to that of a landlord whose tenant is not paying the rent. Your solution is an eviction or unlawful detainer action.

An unlawful detainer action seeks an order from the court granting you possession of the property. Once you have that order, you can seek the assistance of the sheriff in removing the inhabitants and their possessions.

In many states, an unlawful detainer judgment can be obtained in a matter of weeks. It proceeds faster than a quiet title action. Still, if you believe that the inhabitants are going to mount a serious challenge to your title, you may want to combine the unlawful detainer and the quiet title actions, even though the case will then proceed slower.

However you proceed, you cannot put things off for too long, because after a period of years, the inhabitants of your property may attempt to claim title to the property through adverse possession, sometimes called "squatter's rights," and the law of the state may back them up if you sleep on your rights past the statute of limitations.

Obviously, your course of actions is not a do-it-yourself project, even if you happen to be familiar with the state's laws and the county's procedures. Visit a local attorney. One nice thing about having acquired the property as cheaply as you did is that you have a vast amount of equity and have every incentive to do things correctly and thoroughly.

## PRICE THE PROPERTY AGGRESSIVELY

In most parts of the country, we are past the bubble years, when everyone had access to a fortune merely through owning real estate. Your newly acquired property has to compete as an investment with the alternative of selling it and, for example, reinvesting the proceeds in more tax lien certificates. As you have just experienced, that's tough competition for any alternative investment, which would have to clear at least 16% per year, even after expenses. This is unlikely.

You have a lot of equity in your new property. Consider pricing the property low for a quick sale. In every investment, many who begin well but do not fully succeed have fallen prey to the "piggy factor." They push a good thing too far and have to pay the price.

## PAY THE TAXES

I know it sounds bizarre, but some folks who get property through foreclosure on tax lien certificates fail to pay the property taxes. The prior owner has just given you a vivid object lesson. Learn from it.

6%

# Avoiding and Managing Risk

**CHAPTER 14**

# "Worthless" Properties

## WHY THE TAXES WEREN'T PAID

Occasionally,
the owner believes
that he has such a
great use for the
money that causing
the county to make
an involuntary
loan is worth the
interest and penalty
he must pay.

There are a number of reasons why taxes aren't paid. At least initially, people may just forget. But a common reason is that the owner simply does not have enough money for the taxes. Or, more commonly, the money for the taxes is there, but the owner is not able to pay the mortgage and figures that it is not worth paying the taxes just so the bank, rather than the tax collector, takes the property.

Occasionally, the owner believes that he has such a great use for the money that causing the county to make an involuntary loan is worth the interest and penalty he must pay.

Every once in a while, a property owner concludes that the property is simply not worth the taxes. Sometimes he is right. The property could be located on the side of a mountain, under a lake, or next to a rendering plant, or it could be zoned as open space. An additional possibility, one covered in the next chapter, is that the property has an environmental problem. Pima County, Arizona, treasurer Beth Ford warns investors that they can get stuck with properties that are big money losers.[1] For example, she says an investor who holds the tax lien on an old corner gas station could get stuck paying for environmental cleanup if that property is contaminated.[2]

How do you sort out the worthless properties from the gems?

## AVOIDING WORTHLESS PROPERTIES

### Check the Assessments

One of the excellent features of tax lien certificates is that each property comes with a free professional appraisal of its market value by a government agency.

True, the appraisal can be wrong, but if it is grossly wrong, the owner had every incentive to appeal the assessment because the taxes owed were based on the appraisal. Leaving the appraisal unreasonably high and then forfeiting the property because the property is not even worth the taxes would be a wholly illogical reaction.

## Relate the Appraised Value to Appraised Values in the Area

If the assessment appears to be unreasonably low for the area, you should not deal with the property until you have explained the discrepancy. For example, if the property is supposedly improved, but the improvement is appraised at $25,000, you have to assume that there is something wrong with the property or that the structure has only salvage value, in which case it would have to be demolished before you could make any use of the property.

Your aim in checking the assessments is to find an appraised value that appears to be no lower than the appraised values of properties in the area. If it is much lower, it's more likely that there is something wrong with the property than that you have found a great bargain.

In making this comparison, you need to consider the general values in the area of the country where you are dealing. An improved property in a small town in Arizona might be just fine with an appraised value of $60,000. A similar property in urban Connecticut probably would be a disaster.

## Stick with Improved Properties

The rules of wise real estate investing apply to the selection of tax lien certificates. One of the most important of those rules is that raw land is a much more difficult investment to check out than improved land. Because you are buying a tax lien certificate rather than the property itself and are (or ought to be) buying several certificates on different properties, you need to deal with properties that are easy to evaluate.

For the most part, a property has market value because of what can be done with it. Improved property has proven that it has some use; raw land requires a good deal more investigation. The following are a few of the factors that stand in the way of raw land ever being developed:

Raw land is a much more difficult investment to check out than improved land.

ZONING: One of the most obvious reasons that raw land might not ever be improved is that the local government will not allow improvement. This need not be so crude as zoning the property as open space. Zoning a property as residential in the middle of a heavy industrial area will make economic improvement very difficult. Often, there is very good reason why development is restricted, such as the land sits atop an old dump or that a major earthquake fault runs through it.

When you decide to invest in raw land, zoning should be the first thing you check. Nor should you stop there. If the county has a general plan, you should look at that too. It shows not only what the uses of the surrounding land are projected to be, but also what the zoning of the land you are investigating may soon be.

FLOODING: One summer night many years ago, I was driving toward Yosemite National Park when I spotted by moonlight the most beautiful acre of land I had ever seen. The Merced River glistened as it flowed by a white sand beach. Pine trees ringing the land swayed softly in the breeze. I had to have it for a cabin.

The next day, I went to the county recorder's office and explained the location of the land. After a time, the men in the office got a look of recognition and then burst out laughing. "That is a fine looking piece of land, son," one of the men chortled. "We go fishing there pretty often. But in early spring, it's under 10 feet of water!" I knew then that I had a lot to learn.

If you are seriously considering raw land near water, you had best go to the local planning department and see what areas have been designated as floodplains. Next, visit the history section of the local library and try to learn what areas were washed out by big floods.

True, improved land can flood too. But if the improved land is in a neighborhood of improved properties, a lot of people are betting that the improvement will not be washed away. And if the improvement is still there, this is some proof that the property is safe.

WATER RIGHTS: Just as bad as land that floods is land with no access to water. Unless the land is served by a water agency, and that agency confirms that it stands ready to serve this land, you need to provide your own water.

Particularly in the dry Western states, access to a reliable water supply is not assured. If you visit a property in spring and see a

Although seemingly arid lands can often be served by wells, not every property is above usable groundwater.

merry creek gurgling through the property, it is likely that, should you return in September, you will see a dry ditch.

Although seemingly arid lands can often be served by wells, not every property is above usable groundwater, and determining what water is available and who else is laying claim to it can be an expensive and time-consuming process.

SEWAGE DISPOSAL: In developed urban areas, we take sewage disposal for granted. While building your house, you merely hook up to the sewer line that runs down the street.

In many areas, however, there may not be a sewer line, and you are faced with wondering whether the property percolates sufficiently so that a leach field can be installed.

Because you typically do not have access to a property to perform a leaching test before you invest in a tax lien certificate, you must guess about the geology of the site from the experience of neighbors, if there are any.

## Beware of Phony Improvements

*Aaron was thrilled. He had been investing in tax lien certificates for three years but had never actually foreclosed on a property before. Now he had, and he was the proud owner of land improved by a residence in a residential development. Proudly, he drove across the state to see the property he had gotten so cheaply.*

*When Aaron turned around the last bend in the road leading to the property he saw nothing at all! A visit to the local general store revealed that the "residence" was nothing but a mobile home and that although the neighborhood was zoned for a great many more mobile homes, the development had never taken off, but the owner of the property had—with his mobile home! The property, by itself, was almost worthless.*

If I have persuaded you to stick with improved properties, your next task is to be sure that the supposed improvements are real. In the above story, which is entirely true and all too common, the residential neighborhood was worse than a ghost town; at least in a ghost town, the buildings are left behind.

### Be Friends with the County Clerk

In chapter 10, "Getting Local Officials to Help You," I advised you that the surest way to get tax lien certificates on the best properties is to get a local government employee to steer you to the best properties.

Most cities have areas where you wouldn't want to be walking after dark. Some counties have entire towns where you would not want an interest in property. Times Beach, Missouri, comes to mind. It was charming. It had a picturesque setting by the Mississippi River; it was a lovely place, except for the detail that it was contaminated by dioxin and therefore ordered abandoned by the EPA. One town I dealt with as California's toxic waste chief was literally built on deposits of hazardous waste. When my staff tried to warn the residents, they replied hostilely that this was just a "plot" by the next town to annex them.

Problem areas, or even problems with individual properties, are best known by local people. If you are not a local person yourself, it would be a good idea to make the acquaintance of one.

### Diversify

Despite all your precautions, you may eventually meet up with a property that is not even worth the small amount of your tax lien. This is when you lick your wounds and console yourself with the thought of the huge returns you made on the tax lien certificates that paid off for you.

### Look for Hidden Value

In one case with which I am familiar, someone bought a tax lien on an unbuildable strip of land between two nursing homes. Surely it was useless—except to one of the neighbors.

You only need to sell your property to one person. Although it would be fine if a property on which you hold a tax lien certificate were universally appreciated, and although you should definitely seek out properties that are, if you break all the rules and end up in a tight spot, this could be your opportunity to project yourself into the position of potential buyers with special needs.

Some unscrupulous tax lien investors buy liens on otherwise useless properties so they can, for example, block the view of a neighbor, then sell the property to that neighbor for an inflated price so the obstruction can be removed. Such strategies are deplorable,

*Some counties have entire towns where you would not want an interest in property.*

*You only need to sell your property to one person.*

but they illustrate that a property needs to be valuable only to your buyer.

---

**Notes**

1.  Pittman, "County Tax Lien Sale Can Be Risky," *Tucson Citizen,* Business, p. 1D (Feb. 10, 2006).
2.  Ibid.

**CHAPTER 15**

# Environmental Problems

## WHAT PROBLEMS?

### The Good News

For many years, I have been an environmental lawyer, first with the government, then with a large international law firm, and then with my own firm. Based on my knowledge and experience, I can deliver the good news: Buyers of tax lien certificates can avoid environmental liabilities.

Because the rules of environmental liability often are not understood, discussions of real estate–based investments, including tax lien certificates, often are accompanied by vague warnings about environmental problems.

Almost any investment imaginable can be done wrong. But if you follow the basic rule I discuss in this chapter—stick with residential property—you will not be kept up at night by this issue any more than you are about the environmental safety of your own backyard. Those of you who intend to buy tax liens on residential property may skip this chapter. For those with more exotic properties in mind, this chapter is for you.

### The Bad News

The bad news is that those who do suffer environmental liabilities can suffer badly. Each year, owners of private property are forced to commit hundreds of millions of dollars to clean up sites contaminated with hazardous waste and petroleum products from a variety of industrial sources.

According to the EPA, 350,000 contaminated sites will require cleanup over the next 30 years at a cost of as much as $250 billion. The majority of this expenditure will be borne by the owners of the properties (private and public entities) and those potentially responsible for the contamination.

A common misunderstanding is that government funds will clean up this problem. But that's not the case. In fact, for FY 2008, the EPA was funded at $7.5 billion, $264 million less than in FY 2007. Some simple arithmetic will tell you that at those funding levels, it would take hundreds of years to get the job done.

An even more common misunderstanding is that the polluters are being forced to clean up their messes. Although this does occur, it does not occur all that often.

Instead, Congress decided that individual owners and lessees of property should bear the cost of cleanup, even if they did not cause the pollution and had no idea that it was there.[1] This astonishingly unfair idea has been plaguing real estate transactions ever since and has spawned new classes of consultants and expenses. In one famous but happily rare case, a man who bought a building for $380 in back taxes was later informed by the EPA that the property was contaminated and would cost between $600,000 and $1,000,000 to clean up. He was even threatened with a fine of $25,000 for each day he failed to clean up the property.[2]

Two solutions are available to you as a buyer of tax lien certificates: the "physical solution" and the "legal solution." The physical solution refers to the simple actions you should take before getting involved with a property—actions that make it much less likely that the property is polluted in the first place. The legal solution refers to actions you must take to get the advantage of a special exemption Congress has provided to lienholders, including holders of tax lien certificates. In this chapter, I will tell you in detail how to protect yourself in both of these ways.

## THE "PHYSICAL SOLUTION"

### Your Best Protection:
### Stick with Residential Properties

Before I go deeper into this subject, permit me a little redundancy: Limit your tax lien investments to residential properties. In chapter 5, "What to Look for in Properties," you learned that improved residential properties are your best choice if you are looking for a tax lien that will probably be paid off and if you want property

Two solutions are available to you as a buyer of tax lien certificates: the "physical solution" and the "legal solution."

that presents excellent security for the loan. This same advice holds true for avoiding environmental problems.

Even if you were a professional real estate investor, it would not be physically or financially possible for you to send every grain of sand to a hazardous materials laboratory to be absolutely sure that the property is not contaminated. Professional investors therefore select properties that present a minimum possibility that hazardous substances are present. Using that criterion, the property of choice is residential property.

This is not to say that residential property is never contaminated. For example, the infamous Love Canal in New York, where startled property owners began seeing industrial wastes seep into their basements, is a residential community. As an extreme example, in one case I worked on, a couple moved deep into the woods in order to flee civilization, only to find that the land around their rustic cabin had been polluted by the former owner, who made his living salvaging old transformers. Only a volunteer cleanup organized by California's toxic substance control chief (me) saved this couple from financial ruin. In some communities, underground heating oil tanks are common, and these must be considered to be leaking until proven otherwise.

Still, with some exceptions, the possibility of residential property being contaminated is so rare that almost no buyers of residences, nor their even more cautious lenders, pay much attention to it.

If you are cautious, you should ask whether the neighborhood has always been residential. Often you will learn that it has previously been farmland. This presents some possibility that the farmer was overenthusiastic in his use of pesticides. Still, as the property was graded, this problem is often diluted below any level of concern, and the passage of time certainly helps break down many pesticides. As a practical matter, former farmland should not cause worry.

Occasionally, you will learn that the neighborhood is redeveloped industrial land. This would be a good property to skip. Although the chances are good that the developer or the lender checked out the property and that a report by an environmental engineer exists, particularly if the development is recent, you do not normally have the time to evaluate this situation in detail in order to buy a tax lien certificate.

> It [is] not physically or financially possible for you to send every grain of sand to a hazardous materials laboratory to be absolutely sure that the property is not contaminated.

## For Higher-Risk Properties: The Phase 1 Investigation

If you stick with buying tax lien certificates on residential properties, the odds are you will never have environmental problems. Still, fabulous opportunities exist in tax lien certificates on commercial properties. Particularly if your aim is to acquire the properties, you may be considering commercial properties. In that case, I suggest that you do what professional lenders and investors do in this situation: Have a Phase 1 environmental evaluation performed.

A Phase 1 evaluation is designed to confirm that hazardous substances have never been present on a property. It begins by asking about the history of the property. A sample questionnaire is included for your use in appendix III. It covers typical information that an environmental consultant will want to review before beginning a Phase 1 investigation. Once the questionnaire is complete and reveals no history of the presence of hazardous substances, the remainder of the investigation usually consists of at least the following six steps:

1. A trained environmental consultant will walk through the property, looking for signs of environmental problems, such as discolored soil, sickly vegetation, or vent pipes, which indicate the probable presence of underground tanks.
2. Government records will be searched to see whether the property is on one of many lists of contaminated properties or whether a permit for underground tanks has ever been issued for the property.
3. Historical aerial photographs will be searched to see what the use of the property was over the past several decades.
4. Neighbors and former owners of the property will be located and interviewed about activities that occurred on the property.
5. Old business directories will be researched to see what they reveal about past occupants of the property.
6. Title records will be searched to see whether the property ever had an owner with an "industrial-sounding" name.

Your consultant will be aware of and will try to follow as closely as possible more detailed statutory and EPA guidelines for the investigation.

One problem may be obvious: The chances are not good that your consultant will be allowed to conduct a walk-through inspection on private property (unless the property is open to the public). You may have to settle for the observations you can make from a legal vantage point and perhaps redouble your efforts at a record search, for example, by pulling all old business permits issued on a commercial property.

You can expect to spend at least $3,500 for a Phase 1 survey. The investigation will take about three weeks. For about $1,500 more in most parts of the country, you can (and should) hire an environmental lawyer to supervise the investigation. The lawyer can often hire the consultant for less, giving you two experts for the price of one. Furthermore, the lawyer will save you from the worst parts of contracts often used by consultants. Finally, the lawyer will catch and fix problems with draft reports (such as the tendency of some consultants to recommend more work for themselves) and will help preserve the confidentiality of the report.

For those of you who reject this commercial for lawyers, I have also included in appendix III a form contract that you can use in place of your consultant's form contract. Many other forms are found in my book *Environmental Liability and Real Property Transactions* (Aspen Publishers).

Phase 1 investigations are very popular because they are quick and inexpensive. When they bring trouble, it is because they are used in an inappropriate situation. As I mentioned, the purpose of a Phase 1 investigation is to confirm that hazardous substances were never present. If the investigation reveals that hazardous substances were present, the Phase 1 has been flunked, and I suggest you pass.

As is clear from this discussion, a Phase 1 investigation is not feasible for investing in most tax lien certificates. Nor is it necessary if you stick with residential properties.

## For Highest-Risk Properties: The Phase 2 Investigation

The only way you can tell whether hazardous substances were released at a property where they were present is to send representative samples to a laboratory. This process, logically enough, is called a Phase 2 investigation.

In my experience, when a property requires a Phase 2 investigation, it should be considered a risky investment. In many cases, it is hard to know where to take a sample or what to sample for. One

> The purpose of a Phase 1 investigation is to confirm that hazardous substances were never present. If the investigation reveals that hazardous substances were present, the Phase 1 has been flunked, and I suggest you pass.

thing you can be sure of is that a property that requires a Phase 2 investigation will be much more expensive to check out.

The problem of obtaining access to the property is magnified in the case of a Phase 2 investigation. This may not be just a lack of friendliness or a reluctance to have little holes poked in the property or to discourage a possible tax sale. The fact that an environmental consultant is visiting the property may concern the owner that the investigation could reveal a problem, causing a bigger headache for him than the failure to pay back taxes.

## THE "LEGAL SOLUTION"

When Congress passed the so-called Superfund Act,[3] it made all "owners and operators" of property liable for contamination on the property, whether they caused the contamination or not. Lenders were worried. They held liens on properties as security for loans. In some states these mortgages were considered to be the technical ownership of the properties.

In order to avoid being required to clean up the property, lenders persuaded Congress to give lienholders a special exemption from liability. This exemption said that a lienholder is not an "owner or operator" as long as the lender is acting "primarily to protect his security and interest in the property" and as long as the lender is not "participating in the management" of the property.[4]

The limitations on this exemption are of no concern to an investor in a tax lien certificate before there is a foreclosure on the property. A tax lien certificate gives no right to "participate in management" in any way. Furthermore, the only function of a tax lien certificate is to protect the security interest. If you violate the first rule about restricting your tax lien investments to residential properties, you will certainly want to hope that if the property is contaminated, your worst problem will be the loss of your investment and that you will be allowed to cling to a legal loophole while you remain a lienholder.

But what if the taxes and penalties are not paid and you end up owning the property outright? Assuming you had a lienholder's exemption, do you then lose it? No, not if you promptly market the property.

Above all, beware: Environmental laws change quickly, and the cases interpreting them change even more quickly. You need

> In order to avoid being required to clean up the property, lenders persuaded Congress to give lienholders a special exemption from liability.

to consult an expert to update legal advice from this book or any source older than one day.

This is not to say that there is necessarily anything wrong with deciding to keep the property. However, if you plan to hold on to a property, check it out with the same care as though you were buying it on the retail market, using the guidelines for Phase 1 and Phase 2 investigations discussed earlier. If you are dealing with present or former industrial property, you should put a visit to a local environmental consultant on your calendar before you foreclose on the property.

Using the investigation guidelines in this chapter and your own common sense, you can make tax lien certificates as safe as any real estate investment on similar property.

> If you plan to hold on to a property, check it out with the same care as though you were buying it on the retail market.

### Notes

1.  Moskowitz, *Environmental Liability and Real Property Transactions* (John Wiley & Sons, 2d Ed., and Supp. 2008).
2.  Manoil, "Lien Risks Involve Liquidity, Security, Litigation," *Arizona Business Gazette,* International Trade Section, p. 18 (Feb. 3, 1994).
3.  The legal name and citation of this act is the Comprehensive Environmental Response, Compensation and Liability Act, 42 U.S.C. 9601 et seq.
4.  42 U.S.C. 9601(20)A.

## CHAPTER 16

# Bankruptcy

One objection to tax lien certificates that is occasionally raised is that the property owner may declare bankruptcy. For example, *Forbes* darkly reported, "Among the booby traps awaiting investors: a bankruptcy filing by the delinquent taxpayer that wipes out the lien-holder's claims—even though a tax lien is superior to all others."[1]

To call this unclear is an understatement. It is nonsense. The short answer, for those who cannot stand suspense, is that you will be OK. As the holder of a tax lien certificate, you are a secured creditor and a senior creditor. Furthermore, you are a creditor whose lien is almost always a small fraction of the value of the property. You can get your money, with interest, out of this investment.

The major downside of a bankruptcy filing is that it will almost certainly delay your ability to foreclose on the property, sometimes by a few years.

You need to be alert if you get a notice of bankruptcy. You may need to file a claim. However, handled correctly, a declaration of bankruptcy is a bump in the road—an inconvenience but rarely a disaster.

Because this is a subject of some concern, I will briefly summarize the new bankruptcy laws and how they apply to tax lien certificates.

> Handled correctly, a declaration of bankruptcy is a bump in the road— an inconvenience but rarely a disaster.

## THREE TYPES OF BANKRUPTCY

Bankruptcy commonly comes in three forms: Chapter 7, Chapter 11, and Chapter 13. These names refer to the chapters of the Bankruptcy Code that govern these proceedings.

### Chapter 7

Chapter 7 bankruptcy is also known as liquidation bankruptcy. Typically the easiest and fastest form of bankruptcy, it is available to individuals, married couples, corporations, and partnerships. In Chapter 7 the court appoints a trustee who collects and sells your nonexempt property—property the debtor is not allowed to keep—and then uses the proceeds from the sale to pay your creditors.[2]

Under the Bankruptcy Abuse Prevention and Consumer Protection Act of 2005, a debtor must undergo a means test to qualify for Chapter 7 bankruptcy. If the debtor earns too much money to qualify for Chapter 7, he must file for Chapter 13, which requires the debtor to repay a portion of his or her debts over three to five years.[3]

## Chapter 11

Chapter 11 bankruptcy, sometimes called reorganization bankruptcy, is available to individuals, corporations, and partnerships. Unlike Chapter 13 bankruptcy, Chapter 11 has no limits on the amount of debt.[4]

Almost always, the debtor remains in possession of the property and functions much as a trustee would, pursuing remedies and avoiding liabilities.[5] The debtor operates the business under the supervision of the court and for the benefit of creditors.[6]

A committee of unsecured creditors and sometimes additional committees are appointed.[7] These committees investigate the debtor's financial situation and attempt to work out a reorganization plan.[8]

A Chapter 11 plan is confirmed only upon the affirmative votes of the creditors, who are divided by the plan into classes based on the characteristics of their claims and whose votes are a function of the amount of their claims against the debtor.[9]

Ideally, the creditors will agree to the plan. If certain classes of creditors disagree, the plan may be imposed over their objections under certain circumstances. This is known as a cramdown.[10] In either case, if the plan is confirmed by the bankruptcy court, it will govern the rights of the creditors thereafter.

## Chapter 13

Chapter 13 bankruptcy is a repayment plan. Under this chapter, the debtor can propose to pay creditors over three to five years. In order to qualify for Chapter 13 bankruptcy, the debtor needs a stable income with disposable income and must have no more than $922,975 in secured debt and $307,675 in unsecured debt.[11]

The debtor first files a petition in the federal Bankruptcy Court. The debtor must file a Statement of Financial Affairs in addition to a list of creditors, a schedule of assets and liabilities, and a schedule of current income and expenses.[12]

A proposed payment plan must accompany the petition. The proposed payment plan must provide for the payment of all "priority claims"—claims given special status under bankruptcy law such as taxes and the costs of the bankruptcy proceeding—in full unless a particular priority creditor agrees to a different plan.[13] Creditors with no special priority need not, and often do not, get anything under the plan.

The Bankruptcy Court appoints a trustee who will review the proposed plan for accuracy and feasibility. Creditors can object to the plan if they think it is unreasonable. If the plan is approved, the debtor keeps all assets during the period of the plan and makes monthly payments to the trustee, who distributes the money to the creditors according to the plan. If the plan is completed as approved, the debtor is discharged from unpaid debts; if not, several alternatives are open depending on why the plan was not completed.[14]

Under the new law, federal tax returns for the last year must be provided as proof of income in both Chapter 7 and Chapter 13. If the taxes for the prior year have not been paid, the debtor must do so before the bankruptcy can move ahead. In the case of Chapter 13, the debtor must file all tax returns for the previous four years.[15]

There are several nuances of difference between these forms of bankruptcy, but this summary will suit our present purposes.

# THE AUTOMATIC STAY

### Imposing the Stay

Regardless of which type of bankruptcy is chosen, the most important effect of the filing is the immediate and automatic freeze on any actions by creditors to enforce their claims outside the Bankruptcy Court.[16] Indeed, a common reason for the filing of bankruptcy is to obtain an automatic stay on a foreclosure by a secured creditor.

The effect of the automatic stay does not depend on whether you know of the filing. Once the bankruptcy case is filed, any action taken contrary to the automatic stay is given no legal effect and, indeed, must be undone.[17]

The most important effect of the filing is the immediate and automatic freeze on any actions by creditors to enforce their claims.

Once a bankruptcy petition is filed and until the bankruptcy is discharged, the automatic stay is lifted, the property is no longer in the bankruptcy estate, and no action can be taken to enforce a lien on the property,[18] including the foreclosure of a tax lien certificate.

### Lifting the Stay

To ask that the stay be lifted for cause generally requires you to show that the debt is not adequately protected.

Once an automatic stay is in place, there are only two reasons why it might be lifted to allow a secured creditor to foreclose: (1) because the debtor has no equity in the property anyway, so lifting the stay will not affect the distribution of property in bankruptcy, or (2) for cause.[19] To ask that the stay be lifted for cause generally requires you to show that the debt is not adequately protected (meaning that your interest will be somehow harmed by the continuation of the stay).

In most cases, lack of adequate protection for a secured creditor means that the value of the property may not be adequate to cover the value of the claim and that this value might deteriorate further. This is sometimes called the lack of an equity cushion.[20] In the case of a tax lien certificate, where the amount of the debt is usually only a small fraction of the value of the property, it is rare that you can argue the lack of an equity cushion.

In cases where there is not adequate protection for the secured creditor's debt, the Bankruptcy Court will fashion some protection, such as periodic payments to offset the deterioration in value or a lien on other property.[21] Even if there is an adequate equity cushion, where the secured creditor is financially hurt by the continuation of the stay, and where lifting the stay will not harm the debtor or the other creditors, the Bankruptcy Court may decide to lift the stay.[22]

## EXEMPT PROPERTY

Certain types of property are exempt from the reach of creditors in bankruptcy proceedings. Examples are tools of one's trade, health aids, household goods, and a homeowner's exemption in real property.[23]

The exemption of certain property is not of concern in the case of tax liens, however, because a tax lien, notice of which is properly filed, is not subject to exemptions.[24]

# AVOIDANCE OF TRANSFER BY TRUSTEE

## Preferential Transfers

A bankruptcy trustee has the power to cause to be set aside any transfer of property within 90 days of the filing of bankruptcy that preferentially pays one creditor over another of the same class.[25] For example, if a creditor pays a debt owed to his lawyer before declaring bankruptcy, the trustee can set this transfer aside, even though the debt was bona fide.

However, a trustee may not set aside a transfer made pursuant to a valid statutory lien.[26] To be a statutory lien, the lien must be one that would exist regardless of the dependency of bankruptcy or of the debtor's financial condition. Furthermore, it must be a lien that could be asserted against a bona fide purchaser of the property (i.e., one who had no actual knowledge of the lien). Finally, it must not be in favor of a landlord for rent.[27]

A property tax lien, evidenced by a tax lien certificate, fits these requirements: One owes property taxes whether one is rich or poor and whether one is in bankruptcy or not. Because tax obligations are of record, a new buyer of a house could only buy a house subject to the tax lien; the mere sale would not wipe out the lien whether the buyer had actual knowledge of the unpaid taxes or not. Finally, tax liens do not involve a landlord collecting rent. Therefore, if you foreclose on a tax lien certificate, after which the property owner declares bankruptcy, your foreclosure is not subject to being set aside as a preference.

> If you foreclose on a tax lien certificate, after which the property owner declares bankruptcy, your foreclosure is not subject to being set aside as a preference.

The foreclosure of a tax lien often results in the holder of a tax lien certificate receiving a property worth far more than the taxes owed. Still, this does not disadvantage other creditors because the certificate holder would have that right regardless of whether there was a bankruptcy and regardless of what actions other creditors take.

## Fraudulent Transfers

A bankruptcy trustee can set aside a fraudulent transfer made within one year before the bankruptcy filing.[28] When property is bought at a foreclosure sale for less than the supposed fair market value, there are some cases that suggest that this was a fraudulent transfer, even though it involved no collusion with the debtor and even though it makes little sense to talk of the market value of the property as being more than the price actually paid. Other cases disagree.[29]

In Chapter 7 and
Chapter 13 cases,
secured creditors
need not file
proofs of claim . . .
whereas in Chapter
11 cases they must
do so if their claims
are not properly
listed or recognized.

Although this theory seems absurd, that does not mean that some trustee will not try to use it or that some bankruptcy judge will not accept it. The Bankruptcy Court is widely known as the Wild West of legal tribunals, where results are achieved as often with elbows and bluster as with careful legal reasoning.

The result of setting aside a foreclosure sale is that the property will be returned to the estate, and the lien will be restored.[30]

## FILING A PROOF OF CLAIM

The major difference, for our purposes, between the types of bankruptcy is that in Chapter 7 and Chapter 13 cases, secured creditors need not file proofs of claim, although under some circumstances they may want to do so, whereas in Chapter 11 cases, they must do so if their claims are not properly listed or recognized.

Thus, in a Chapter 7 case, only unsecured creditors must file a proof of claim.[31] This rule has no application to the holder of a tax lien certificate because the claim is secured by the property.[32]

In a Chapter 11 case, the debtor prepares a list of claims and interests in his property. Any person whose claims or interests are listed in the proper amount and whose claims and interests are not described as disputed, contingent, or unliquidated (i.e., are in an unknown amount) does not need to file a proof of such claims and interests.[33] The creditor's filing must be made before a date set (and can be extended) by the Bankruptcy Court. This date is known as the bar date.[34]

In a Chapter 11 case, you are in worse shape if the debtor puts down your lien for the wrong amount than if he never lists you at all. There is authority that if you are absent from the debtor's list, your lien will survive the Chapter 11 proceeding, even if you do not file, but you will be bound by errors in the debtor's listing.[35] Because you will not usually see the debtor's list, the sensible course will be to file a proof of interest in the proper form before the bar date, attaching the tax lien certificate.[36]

In a Chapter 13 case, as in a Chapter 7 case, a secured creditor need not file a proof of claim unless the claim is challenged.[37]

# COLLECTION OF INTEREST AFTER FILING OF BANKRUPTCY

When the property is worth more than a secured claim, the creditor is entitled to interest on the claim. The property securing a tax lien certificate is almost always worth far more than the taxes due. You will therefore be entitled to interest on the debt.[38] However, this interest may not be at the same rate you were earning under state law.[39]

# PUTTING IT TOGETHER: DEALING WITH BANKRUPTCY

We can conclude from this discussion that the possibility that a property owner will go into bankruptcy is a manageable risk. As long as a timely proof of claim is sent to the clerk of the Bankruptcy Court in a Chapter 11 case, the investment is secure. You do not even need to do this in a Chapter 7 or Chapter 13 case. The automatic stay will delay your foreclosure until the bankruptcy is over, but in the meantime, you could get some interest.

All things considered, you would rather not deal with a property that is tied up in a bankruptcy. Therefore, if you happen to know that a property owner is or will be in bankruptcy, you should stay away from a tax lien on the property because the bankruptcy will reduce your liquidity.

Checking the Bankruptcy Court files in the owner's district of residence is a possible precaution. However, the owner could always declare bankruptcy after the sale.[40] Considering the overall statistical and tactical risk posed by bankruptcy and the number of properties you will be dealing with, this level of diligence may not be cost-effective.

Above all, keep in mind that the law changes constantly. Do not rely much on your memory of it or on any summary, including this one. If you actually care about the application of the law to your situation, consult an expert.

> The possibility that a property owner will go into bankruptcy is a manageable risk.

### Notes

1. Lubove, "Caveat Emptor," *Forbes,* p. 80 (Dec. 24, 1990).
2. "Chapter 7 Bankruptcy Basics," http://bankruptcy.lawyers.com/Chapter-7-Bankruptcy-Basics.html.
3. Ibid.
4. "Chapter 11," http://www.moranlaw.net/chapter11.htm.
5. Ibid.
6. Ibid.
7. Ibid.
8. Ibid.
9. Ibid.
10. Ibid.
11. "Chapter 13 Bankruptcy Tax Tool," http://bankruptcy.lawyers.com/Chapter-13-Bankruptcy-Tax-Tool.html.
12. Ibid.
13. Ibid.
14. Ibid.
15. Ibid.
16. 11 U.S.C. 362, 922.
17. Ginzberg, *Bankruptcy: Text, Statutes, Rules* ("Ginzberg"), pp. 198–199, 3.01[b] [1] and [2] (1989 and 1991 Supp.).
18. 11 U.S.C. 362(a) (3)–(5).
19. Ibid., 362(d).
20. Ginzberg, supra, p. 248, 1305[e].
21. Ibid., p. 247, 3.05[d][l].
22. Ibid., pp. 252–253, 1305Lfl.
23. 11 U.S.C. 522.
24. Ibid., 522(c)(3); 5 Collier, *Bankruptcy Practice Guide* ("Collier"), pp. 74–78, 74.02 [5] (1992).
25. Ibid., 547.
26. Ibid., 547(c)(6).
27. 11 U.S.C. 545. 33.
28. Ibid., 548.
29. Ginzberg, supra, pp. 694–696, 9.03[g]; 2 Cowans, *Bankruptcy Law and Practice* ("Cowans"), p. 219, 10.9.
30. 11 U.S.C. 548(c).
31. Fed. Rules of Bankr. Proc. 3002(a).
32. 11 U.S.C. 548(c).
33. Ibid., 1111(a).
34. Fed. Rules of Bankr. Proc. 3002(a).

35. Lopucki, *Strategies for Creditors in Bankruptcy Proceedings,* p. 731, 12.7 (2nd Ed. 1991).

36. 5 Collier, supra, pp. 88-21–88-23, 88.11[3][c] (1992).

37. Ginzberg, supra, p. 779, 10.07[e].

38. 11 U.S.C. 506(b); 2 Cowans, supra, p. 602, 12.32 (1991) [involuntary lien entitled to interest].

39. Ibid., p. 606, 12.32.

**CHAPTER 17**

# Scams

Considering the fabulous legitimate opportunities presented by tax lien certificates and the relative ease of purchasing them, it seems improbable that they would be fodder for consumer fraud. At least it seems improbable until one reflects on the endless ingenuity of con artists and the equally endless gullibility of their victims.

In the case of tax lien certificates, the high value represented by the properties coupled with the low cost of the investment creates a spread that is ripe for a creative sales pitch.

So it was that in Milwaukee, a fellow named Melvyn gathered together members of the Hmong refugee community and invited them to join the International Loan Network for a mere $225. This cost allowed them to become a "DaddyTom" and get part of similar fees paid by new recruits. According to their own estimates, some 40,000 people joined this group.[1]

For another $400, you got the right to join the "$1,000 Property Rights Assignment Program," which entitles you (if you pay an additional $250 processing fee) to have assigned to you a tax lien certificate on property with an assessed value of no less than $10,000.[2]

That might sound good for half a second, until you reflect that the last tax lien certificate I bought cost me $1,300, and the assessed value of the property was $40,000. This implies that the lien on the $10,000 property could easily have cost the promoters only $325.

If you like that investment, though, you would love the opportunity to pay $5,000 for a tax lien certificate on property assessed at more than $50,000 or a $10,000 certificate on property assessed at more than $100,000. Naturally, the additional "processing fee" on these bigger transactions is raised to $500.[3]

Odd as this deal was, apparently 162 people in Milwaukee bought tax lien certificates this way on property that they knew nothing about. One tax lien investor rightly called this buying "a pig in a poke."[4] An expensive pig at that.

The Securities and Exchange Commission took an interest in this plan and obtained a preliminary injunction. It told a U.S. court of appeals that this pyramid scheme violated securities laws and that the sales were made without adequate disclosures.[5]

Obviously, if you are reading chapter 17 of this book, you would not have gotten caught up in such a plan. No "entry fee" is needed to buy tax lien certificates, and there is no need to vastly overpay for them. So this chapter is not so much a warning as something for us to marvel at together.

When tax lien certificates enter the mainstream of investment interest, no doubt regulations specific to them will follow, as has been the case with stocks, bonds, mutual funds, and commodities. At the moment, the best that can be said is that if you don't buy your tax lien certificates directly from the government, having done your own homework, then delegate the buying only to a person you trust entirely, and verify through the county treasurer that what you are buying is genuine.

Of course, this does not mean that delegating the time and bother of investigating and buying the certificates has no value. True, an experienced tax lien investor who commented on the International Loan Network said, "Why pay someone else to do something you can do yourself at no cost?"[6] I suppose that means that his wife cuts his hair. There is plenty of reason to pay people to do things you could do yourself. Just make sure you pay the right people the right price for the right service.

A fully developed market will save you time and will give you access to professional managers and recordkeepers. This will be a convenience and a welcome development. And it will almost certainly be a better bargain than the International Loan Network.

---

**Notes**

1. Kendall, "Investment Network Targets Area Poor, Promises Control of Money," *The Business Journal of Milwaukee* (Jan. 28, 1991).

2. Ibid.

3. Ibid.

4. Ibid.

5. Bureau of National Affairs, "SEC Urges Appeals Court to Affirm Injunction in ILN Investment Scheme," 24 Securities Regulation and Law Report 683 (May 8,1992).

6. Kendall, supra.

**CHAPTER 18**

# FDIC Liens

A number of banks have failed in recent times because they have made loans on overvalued properties to underqualified borrowers. When a bank fails, loans owed to the bank are administered by the Federal Deposit Insurance Corporation (FDIC). Usually, such a bank is quickly acquired by another bank under federal supervision. Sometimes, however, there is a significant delay in this process. When you know that a lender that holds a mortgage on a property has been taken over by the FDIC, you would do well to avoid a tax lien certificate on that property.

In addition, if you plan to foreclose on a tax lien certificate you already own, check to see who the lender is and whether the lender has been taken over by the FDIC. If you discover that it has been, hold off on foreclosing on the tax lien until a successor has taken over, unless you want to try to obtain the agency's consent. It will do you little good to own a property subject to the assertion of the FDIC lien, and you can hardly afford to litigate this sort of dispute, given the small amount of money you are likely to have at risk.

If you purchased a tax lien certificate before the FDIC took over the property, or if the FDIC has a lien interest in the property and the tax lien has priority over the FDIC lien, and if the FDIC wants to eliminate your interest in the property, it will pay the amount required by state law to satisfy such interest (other than any fees or penalties specifically imposed to redeem such interest). If the tax lien does not have priority, the FDIC will take whatever action is necessary to ensure that its own interest is satisfied first.[1]

Special care must be taken, however, in states that require foreclosure in a short period of time, such as two years in Maryland and three years in Iowa. This can create a dilemma in which awaiting resolution of the federal lien issue could push you over the state's deadline for foreclosure.

**Note**

1.    FDIC Statements of Policy (12-31-96, p. 5331).

16%

# Appendices

# Chart of State Laws

| STATE | RATE OF INTEREST | REDEMPTION PERIOD | NUMBER OF COUNTIES | NOTES |
|---|---|---|---|---|
| Alabama | 12% | 3 years | 67 | |
| Arizona | 16% | 3 years | 15 | Foreclosure a little easier after 5 years |
| Colorado | fluctuates | 3 years | 64 | 9% above federal discount rate |
| Florida | 18% | 2 years | 67 | |
| Georgia | 10% | 1 year | 159 | |
| Illinois | 18%+ | 2½ years | 102 | |
| Indiana | 10–25% | 1 year | 92 | |
| Iowa | 24% | 1¾ years | 99 | Foreclosure required in 3 years |
| Kentucky | 12% | 3 years | 120 | |
| Louisiana | 17% | 3 years | 64 | Rate is 12% after first year |
| Maryland | varies | 2–6 months | 23 | Foreclosure required in 2 years. Baltimore pays 24% |
| Massachusetts | 16% | 2½ years | 14 | |
| Mississippi | 18% | 2 years | 82 | |
| Missouri | 10% | 1 year | 114 | |
| Nebraska | 14% | 3 years | 93 | |
| New Hampshire | 18% | 2 years | 10 | |
| New Jersey | 18% + 2–6% | 2 years | 21 | Foreclosure required in 20 years |
| New York | 14% | 2 years | 62 | Only in some counties |
| Oklahoma | 8% | 2 years | 77 | |
| South Carolina | 8–12% | 1–1½ years | 46 | |
| Vermont | 12% | 1 year | 14 | |
| West Virginia | 12% | 17 months | 55 | |
| Wyoming | 18% | 4 years | 23 | Foreclosure required in 6 years |
| | | | Total = 1,483 | |

# The 16% Winner's Circle

Although this book has so far given you an overview of how to buy, collect on, and foreclose tax lien certificates, if you are ready to roll up your sleeves and try what you have learned in a particular state, you will need to study the details of that state's laws.

In this appendix, I have selected the states that pay 16% or more on their tax lien certificates. In addition, I have included a few more because they are temporarily paying only slightly below that rate or because they illustrate some interesting variation in procedures. This appendix, then, gives you a close-up view of the winners.

For each state, I have included several up-to-date Web sites for the most prominent and promising local jurisdictions. But Web sites change often. To minimize misfires, I have often provided the more general site, from which you can then navigate to the treasurer, tax collector, or tax lien sale or fill in "tax sale" in the search box.

For those of you who want to review the full text of the original statutes in a law library or to make sure that no changes in the law have occurred since this book was published, I have noted some helpful citations in the margin to get you started.

## ARIZONA

### When Taxes Are Delinquent

One-half of the yearly property taxes is considered delinquent in Arizona if they remain unpaid after November 1 at 5:00 p.m. The other half is delinquent if not paid by May 1 at 5:00 p.m. If those days are not business days, then the deadline is 5:00 p.m. on the next business day.

§§ 42-18051–42-18403 (all references are to Arizona Revised Statutes)

§ 42-18052

§ 42-18053    Until these taxes are paid, a penalty is assessed of "sixteen per cent per year simple until paid," and "a fraction of a month is counted as a whole month."

§ 42-18102    The county treasurer shall maintain a record of delinquent taxes, listing the properties, owners of record, and amount of taxes, penalties, and interest due.

### Advertising the Sale of Tax Lien Certificates

In Arizona, the sale of tax lien certificates is not a matter of local option. Rather:

§ 42-18104    *(B) The county treasurer shall advertise and sell the tax lien for the aggregate amount of all unpaid taxes that are delinquent on the property, together with all penalties, interest and charges respectively due for the current or preceding years, whether or not the aggregate amount or any part has been reduced to judgment.*

§ 42-18106    On or before December 31 of each year the county treasurer shall prepare a list of all real property on which the taxes for prior tax years are unpaid and delinquent, describing the property as it is described on the tax roll. He will also prepare an accompanying notice stating that the treasurer will sell a tax lien on each parcel of real property at public auction for taxes, penalties, interest, and charges on the real property.

§ 42-18109    The county treasurer will post a correct copy of the list and auction notice near the outer door of the office. The list and notice shall remain posted for at least two weeks before the date of the sale. He must also give notice to the delinquent owner. The county treasurer must also advertise the list and notice at least once in a newspaper of general circulation in the county between two and three weeks before the sale. In addition, the newspaper that prints the list and notice shall also post the list and notice from the first publication date through March 1 of the current year on the Internet on a Web site that posts the legal notices of 10 or more Arizona newspapers.

### Tax Lien Auction

§ 42-18112    The tax lien sale is held in February of each year. All liens are put up for sale. If no bid is made on a lien, the treasurer tries to sell it each following day, Sundays and holidays excluded, until the tax lien on each parcel has been sold.

If there is no bid for a tax lien, the county treasurer can offer it again at the beginning of the sale on the next day until all tax liens are sold or until he becomes satisfied that no more sales can be made.

§ 42-18113

A real property tax lien shall be awarded to the person who pays the whole amount of delinquent taxes, interest, penalties, and charges due on the property and who in addition offers to accept the lowest rate of interest on the amount so paid to redeem the property from the sale, which may not exceed "sixteen per cent per year simple until paid," and "a fraction of a month is counted as a whole month."

§ 42-18114

The entire amount of the bid must be paid in cash at the time of the sale. After the sale, the tax lien certificate is issued for a fee of not more than $10.

§ 42-18116

## Buying Unsold Tax Liens

If a tax lien is not sold, it is assigned to the state, and the county treasurer will sell the certificate of purchase to any person who pays the whole amount of the taxes, including interest, penalties, and charges. A tax lien certificate bought this way will yield the full 16% maximum without the competition of an auction.

§ 42-18122

## Lost Tax Lien Certificates, Assignments

If a certificate of purchase is lost, it can be replaced if the buyer supplies a notarized affidavit and $5 fee.

§ 42-18120

If a person who holds a certificate of purchase does not exercise the option to purchase the certificate, the county treasurer "may require a person who desires to purchase a subsequent certificate of purchase on the property to acquire by assignment all currently outstanding certificates of purchase previously issued on the property. The county treasurer shall process the sale as an assignment on behalf of the previous holder of the certificate of purchase."

§ 42-18121-01

## Paying Subsequent Years' Taxes

Once you have a tax lien certificate, you may decide to pay the following years' taxes when they, too, become delinquent. The advantages of this are that this additional money starts earning high interest, you avoid the auction, and you solidify your position as the sole lienholder in case the property is foreclosed.

§ 42-18121

*On or after June 1, if a person who holds a certificate of purchase desires to pay subsequent taxes, accrued interest and related fees due on the property, the person shall exhibit the certificate or receipt of registered certificate to the county treasurer. The treasurer shall enter the amount of the payment on the certificate and on the record of tax lien sales.*

A $5 fee is charged for this transaction.

## Payment of Certificate Holder

§ 42-18152

A real property tax lien may be redeemed at any time within three years after the date of sale but before the delivery of a treasurer's deed to the purchaser or the purchaser's heirs or assigns.

§ 42-18155

As soon as the property owner redeems, the county treasurer will pay the lienholder on demand the amount owed upon surrender of the tax lien certificate. If only a portion of the lien is paid (for example, by a person who owns less than the entire property), the tax lien certificate will be endorsed with the portion paid.

## Foreclosing on a Tax Lien

§ 42-18201

*At any time beginning three years after the sale of a tax lien but not later than ten years after the last day of the month in which the lien was acquired, if the lien is not redeemed, the purchaser or the purchaser's heirs or assigns . . . may bring an action to foreclose the right to redeem.*

§ 42-18204

The foreclosure action results in a judgment "directing the county treasurer to expeditiously execute and deliver to the party in whose favor judgment is entered . . . a deed conveying the property described in the certificate of purchase. After entering judgment, the parties whose rights to redeem the tax lien are thereby foreclosed have no further legal or equitable right, title, or interest in the property subject to the right of appeal and stay of execution as in other civil actions."

§ 42-18206

The property owner can still dash in after the foreclosure action is brought but before the judgment is issued and redeem the property, but if he waits that long, he must also pay the costs and reasonable attorney's fees of the tax lienholder who is foreclosing.

§ 42-18261

Instead of foreclosing in court after three years, the holder of the tax lien certificate can decide to wait five years. At that time, the lienholder can simply go to the county treasurer and apply for and receive a treasurer's deed to the property. This process also requires notice to the property owner and posting of the property.

Whatever process is used, the result is a brand new treasurer's deed to the property.

§ 42-18267

## Local Variations

Although the basic procedures are set by state law, each county has its own variations. The following is the explanation of the tax lien procedures published by Maricopa County, where Phoenix is located (see http://www.treasurer.maricopa.gov/research/tutorial/tutorial.htm). You will notice some details not covered in the state statutes previously summarized.

## TAX LIEN INFORMATION

### AUCTION

The Tax Lien Sale provides for the payment of delinquent property taxes by an investor. The tax on the property is auctioned in open competitive bidding based on the least percent of interest to be received by the investor.

Property taxes that are delinquent at the end of December are added to any previously uncollected taxes on a parcel for the Tax Lien Sale. The sale takes place in February of each year. Please read the disclaimer before deciding to bid, and see our lien FAQ page and lien history page.

Parcels whose taxes are subject to sale will be advertised, in January, in a Maricopa County newspaper of general circulation. They are listed by sequence number. Parcels fall into 1 of 2 groups. Each group is sorted by parcel number.

The advertisement appears about three weeks before the auction and is also posted on the Internet.

Copies of the newspaper are usually available for purchase at the Treasurer's Office. In addition a CD of those parcels can also be purchased.

The investor is responsible for all research on the parcels available for auction. County maps for research may be obtained by visiting the Maricopa County Assessor's Office. Read our Recommendations to all bidders.

PRE-SALE REQUIREMENTS

To be eligible to bid, investors must provide the Treasurer's Office with a completed Bidder Information Card and Request for Taxpayer Identification Number and Certification (IRS Form W-9 or W-8).

A number will be assigned to each bidder for use when purchasing tax liens.

PROXY BID PROCEDURE

In a live auction, a bidder will lower his bid by one percent increments until he is the only bidder left or until the interest goes below his acceptable minimum level, at which point he would drop out. Proxy bidding is a form of competitive sale in which bidders enter the minimum interest rate that they are willing to accept for each certificate. The auction system acts as an electronic agent, submitting bids on behalf of each bidder. The result of the proxy system is that the electronic agent keeps lowering the bid to submit by one percent increments until you are either the only bidder left (in which case you get the certificate at one percent lower than the previous bid) or until you reach the floor you have set. Zero percent bids will not be treated as proxy bids. They will be awarded at zero.

If you are the only bidder on a given certificate and your minimum rate is greater than zero percent, the electronic agent will submit a bid of 16% on your behalf.

In the case of a tie at the winning bid rate, the system awards to one of the tie bidders through a random selection process using a random number generator.

In no case will a bidder be awarded a certificate at a rate lower than his specified minimum acceptable rate.

Certificates that receive no bids will be "struck to the state" at 16%.

The successful bidder will pay the entire amount of taxes, interest, and fees via ACH debit by the end of the next business day. If payment has not been made the parcel(s) may be re-offered.

The sale will continue until all liens are sold or the lack of bidding warrants discontinuing the sale.

Each investor will receive a Sale Portfolio Report identifying each parcel for which the investor had acquired a tax lien.

When making an inquiry on a property, use the parcel number located in the left column of the Portfolio.

## BID INTEREST

Bids must be on the basis of interest income to bidder.

The maximum bid is 16% simple interest per annum, prorated monthly. The lowest acceptable bid is 0% per annum.

The successful (lowest) bid will determine the rate of interest to be paid on the Tax Lien, representing the amount of taxes, interest, fees and charges then due.

## REDEMPTION OF LIENS

If the owner and/or agent redeems the property, the investor receives a payment of what they paid for the lien, less the processing fee, plus the prorated monthly rate of interest that was awarded at the sale.

## DEEDS

When a property owner fails to redeem the CP prior to the expiration of three years from the date the parcel was first offered at sale, the investor may apply for a court ordered deed to the property (judicial foreclosure).

As of December 31, 2003, the Treasurer's Office does not issue Treasurer's deeds on buyer purchased CPs. All buyer foreclosures are judicial.

## ASSIGNMENTS

Assignments offer the investor an alternative way to purchase liens on parcels at a time other then the Tax Lien sale.

The unsold parcels "struck off to state" (State CPs) at the Tax Lien sale are available to investors by assignment. Assignments will be available upon completion of all Sale Week transactions.

Assignment purchases may be made in person or by mail. Payment must accompany the request. Available parcels are listed as "STATE CP" on a printout located in the Client Services Department of the Treasurer's Office

This listing is available for purchase in two forms, printout or diskette, for $50 each. It lists the tax amount and year involved. The buyer will pay the entire amount of taxes, interest, and fees due at the date of the assignment. Assignment purchases are not allowed during the tax sale auction. NOTE: If a parcel also has current delinquent taxes in addition to "State CP" taxes, the investor may purchase both after June 1, and prevent the parcel from going to the Tax Lien Sale.

### ASSIGNMENT PURCHASING

The buyer will submit a list of desired parcels to the Treasurer's Office, along with a cashier's check, money order, certified check, or wire transfer for the approximate total. The submittals will be recorded and processed in the order in which they are received. Should the original payment be in excess of the amount due, a refund will be issued.

Assignment purchases are processed up to the amount received.

Parcels not covered by funds on hand are available to other buyers. The interest earned on an assignment will be the current statutory maximum (16%).

"Assignment" must be specified to prevent an inadvertent processing of a redemption of a Certificate of Purchase.

## SUBTAX

Subsequent Tax (Subtax) can be added to an existing lien to protect the investor's fiduciary interest. The subtaxing of the current year's taxes onto an existing lien begins June 1 and ends January 31. All remaining taxes go to the Tax Lien Sale in February.

The investor is responsible for the research of the parcel's unpaid taxes. The subtax consists of taxes, interest, and fees dependent on the date the taxes are being paid. There is an additional $5.00 fee for each purchase submitted for subtax to be applied for each year requested.

The payment procedure for a subtax is the same as for assignments. The interest earned on a subtax is the same as that of the original CP.

## TRANSFER OF CERTIFICATES OF PURCHASE

If not redeemed, a CP may be transferred by affidavit to another person who has a Bidder Identification Card on file with the Treasurer's Office.

There is a $10.00 transfer fee.

The Treasurer's Office must be notified of the transfer for it to be valid. The Treasurer pays the redeemed taxes to the last CP holder on record.

## MONTHLY ACTIVITY STATEMENTS

An Activity Statement will be sent to each CP buyer listing their redemptions, purchases, and surrenders. Statements will only be sent to those accounts with activity in the last month.

## IMPORTANT TELEPHONE NUMBERS

Treasurer's Customer Service . . . . . . . (602) 506-8511
Personal Property . . . . . . . . . . . . . . (602) 506-3386
Assessor's Office . . . . . . . . . . . . . . (602) 506-3406

### INTERNET

PARCEL RESEARCH REQUEST
treasurer.maricopa.gov/researchrequest
TAX GUIDE
http://www.treasurer.maricopa.gov/taxguide.htm

**Maricopa County Treasurer**
**301 West Jefferson Room 100**
**Phoenix, AZ 85003-2199**

**http://www.treasurer.maricopa.gov/**
**treasurer@mail.maricopa.gov**

POST SALE NOTE
The Treasurer's Office is PAPERLESS; this means Certificates are no longer printed. At the end of the sale, you will receive an itemized listing of what you bid on via email.

## Web Sites

The following are some URLs and contact information for tax lien sale information for other counties in Arizona:
APACHE COUNTY: http://www.co.apache.az.us/treasurer/copprocedure.html
COCONINO COUNTY: http://www.coconino.az.gov/index.aspx
GILA COUNTY: http://www.co.gila.az.us/treasurer/default.html
GRAHAM COUNTY: http://www.graham.az.gov/Graham_CMS/default.aspx

GREENLEE COUNTY: http://www.co.greenlee.az.us/Treasurer/
   TreasurerHomePage.aspx
MOHAVE COUNTY: http://www.co.mohave.az.us/default.aspx
NAVAJO COUNTY: http://www.navajocountyaz.gov/treasurer/
PIMA COUNTY: http://www.to.co.pima.az.us/
PINAL COUNTY: http://pinalcountyaz.gov/Departments/
   Treasurer/Pages/Home.aspx
YAVAPAI COUNTY: http://www.co.yavapai.az.us/Treasurer.aspx
YUMA COUNTY: http://www.co.yuma.az.us/treas/index.htm

**Telephone Numbers and E-Mail Addresses**
COCHISE COUNTY TREASURER: (520) 432-8400
   treasurer@co.cochise.az.us
LA PAZ COUNTY TREASURER: (928) 669-6145
SANTA CRUZ COUNTY TREASURER: (520) 375-7980
   cramirez@co.santa-cruz.az.us

# COLORADO

Tax lien auctions in most states award the winning bid to the person willing to accept the lowest rate of interest. Colorado is more pragmatic. In Colorado, you have the winning bid if you are willing to fork over the most cash to the state. You cannot get too enthusiastic about this process, however, because any extra money you pay will not be returned even if the property owner redeems. This is simply another way of lowering the interest rate, except that the county, rather than the delinquent property owner, benefits from the competition.

Although the statutes talk of a sale of the properties, in fact, the buying of a "Certificate of Purchase" does not allow possession until the expiration of the redemption period.

Unlike in other states, where the interest rate is fixed, the rate of interest the delinquent property owner must pay is changed each year to be 9% above the best rate a bank can get from the Federal Reserve. For example, if the discount rate is 4%, you will earn 13%.

**Notification of Sale**
September 1 of each year, taxpayers are notified if their taxes are delinquent. The notice shall indicate the amount the taxpayer

§§ 39-11-101,
39-11-102

owes and tell the taxpayer that if the money is not paid by the date specified in the notice, which shall not be less than 15 days from the date of mailing of the notice, the treasurer will advertise and sell a tax lien on the person's property on the date specified in the notice at public auction for the delinquent taxes, interest, and applicable fees.

Next, the sale of the properties is advertised in three issues of a weekly newspaper, the first to be published at least four weeks before the date of the sale. If the notice is advertised in a daily newspaper, the notice will be published three times, one day a week, for three weeks, on the same day. The notice will also be posted in the treasurer's office for not less than four weeks before the date of sale.

## Conduct of the Sale

§§ 39-11-108, 39-11-109

The tax sale is held on or before the second Monday in December of each year. The sale continues from day to day, except for Saturday and Sunday, until all the certificates are sold or until it is evident that they will not be sold.

§§ 39-11-111, 39-11-115

When the treasurer sells any tax lien on any lands or lots for delinquent taxes, the treasurer may accept payment of the purchase price in the form of cash, negotiable paper, or electronic funds transfer, subject to the treasurer's bidding rules.

The certificates are sold to "the persons who pay therefore the taxes, delinquent interest, and fees then due thereon or who further pay the largest amount in excess of said taxes, delinquent interest, and fees." The excess amount shall be credited to the county general fund. Each tax lien shall be sold for an entire piece of property.

Each county can make its own rules about the minimum bid increase and the order of bidding.

§ 39-11-117

The successful bidder will get a "Certificate of Purchase," which indicates the rate of interest.

For information about the date of the sale and details about local procedures, contact the county beginning in December.

## Assignment of Certificates

§ 39-11-118

Certificates of purchase are "assignable by endorsement." If the assignment is registered, the buyer gets all rights and title of the original purchaser.

## Lost Certificates

If a Certificate of Purchase is lost, upon presentation of satisfactory evidence, a new one will be issued.

§ 39-11-120

## Payment of the Following Years' Taxes

The holder of a Certificate of Purchase may present the certificate and pay delinquent taxes for the following year. The additional payment earns interest at the same rate as does the original purchase.

§ 39-11-119

## Redemption by Property Owner

At any time before a Treasurer's Deed is issued, as described below, the property owner can redeem the property by paying costs and interest at a rate "nine percentage points above the discount rate, which discount rate shall be the rate of interest a commercial bank pays to the Federal Reserve Bank of Kansas City using a government bond or other eligible paper as security, and shall be rounded to the nearest full percent." This rate is determined on September 1 and becomes effective October 1.

§ 39-12-103

If the property owner redeems, the holder of the Certificate of Purchase is paid upon surrender of the certificate.

§ 39-12-109

## Obtaining a Treasurer's Deed

If the property owner does not redeem, three years from the date of sale and upon presentation of the Certificate of Purchase, the treasurer shall make out a deed.

§ 39-11-120

Before doing this, though, the treasurer will serve the people in actual possession of the property and the people on the tax roll by personal service or, if necessary, by either registered or certified mail. This notice will not be more than five months or less than three months before the deed is issued. In addition, notice will be published at three weekly intervals.

§ 39-11-128

## Void Deeds and Certificates

If the treasurer makes a mistake (for example, if the taxes were really paid but not properly credited), the buyer will be paid interest by the county, only at 2% above the set discount rate to the nearest percentage point but no lower than 8%.

§ 39-12-111

The statute of limitations for the property owner to attack a Treasurer's Deed is five years after its issuance. This can be up to

§§ 39-12-101, 39-12-104, 39-11-133

nine years under certain circumstances, however. You can bring a "quiet title" action (a lawsuit to confirm that you have good title) to cut short this possibility.

§ 39-11-104

If you lose the property, you may have a claim for improvements you made to it.

### Local Variations

The following is an explanation by the San Miguel County Treasurer, located in Telluride, of how tax lien certificates are issued in this county.

# SAN MIGUEL COUNTY TREASURER
**Phone: 970-728-4451**
**Fax: 970-728-4397**
**P.O. Box 488**
**Telluride, CO 81435**
**http://www.sanmiguelcounty.org/portal/page?_**
**pageid=117,144871&_dad=portal&_schema=PORTAL**

THE TAX LIEN SALE TAKES PLACE
THE LAST MONDAY IN NOVEMBER.

## Who Can Participate?

No tax lien shall be sold to an elected or appointed county official, to a county employee, or to a member of the immediate family of such person or to the agent of any such county official or employee during the time the official or employee holds office or is employed.

REGISTRATION

Registration begins at 9:00 a.m. the morning of the sale. It is imperative that a W-9 form is completed and on file with our office. Individuals will not be allowed to participate in our Tax Lien Sale without a completed W-9.

### IRS REQUIREMENTS

We are required by the Internal Revenue Service to issue 1099-INT Forms to tax lien buyers. You must complete a W-9 at time of registration or have one on file with the San Miguel County Treasurer's Office to participate in our Tax Lien Sale.

### INTEREST RATE

Interest rate is 9 points above the discount rate on September 1st each year.

### BUYER'S LIST

A current buyer's list can be picked up at the registration table on Tax Lien Sale day.

### ORDER OF SALE

Properties will be sold by item number, which is listed in alphabetical order by owner's name. All tax liens are sold and issued on the day of the sale.

### STRIKE-OFFS

Anyone with a legal interest in a particular parcel(s) and desiring a lien stricken off to them must sign a declaration of legal vested interest and deposit the dollar amount to cover these liens prior to the tax lien sale. We will announce these strike-offs at the beginning of the Tax Lien Sale. If other buyers do not object to the strike-off requests, the sale of these liens will be considered final.

### PREMIUM BIDS

Premium bids are those in excess of the advertised dollar amount. On parcels listed at $500 or more, the minimum raise is $10.00. On parcels listed under $500, the minimum raise is $1.00. All premium bids are made at

INVESTOR'S EXPENSE and ABSOLUTELY NO INTEREST IS EARNED on them, nor is this amount refunded when the property is redeemed.

## END OF SALE AND PAYMENT

Purchase must be paid before leaving the premises. FAILURE TO DO SO WILL RESULT IN LOSS OF LIENS PURCHASED!

Verify account expenditure with the account balance clerk located at the Tax Lien Sale registration counter. Your bidder card MUST be dropped off at check out. Make checks payable to: San Miguel County Treasurer. Checks must be made for the exact amount of purchases.

## TAX LIEN CERTIFICATES OF SALE

All certificates of sale will be held in safekeeping in the San Miguel County Treasurer's vault unless otherwise instructed by a formal written request. A safekeeping receipt and complete computer report of all Tax Lien Sale purchases will be forwarded to you. This usually takes about 7–10 working days; this process will not be completed until the bidder card is returned.

## AFTER THE SALE

Three years following the date of Tax Lien Sale, an application for a Treasurer's Deed may be accepted from the tax lien holder if redemption of the lien is not received. The application process ranges from five to six months. All legally interested parties are given a 120-day redemption period to keep their interest in the property. Deed applications involves: remittance of $500.00 deposit to cover fees for advertising, certified mailings, title searches, and miscellaneous legal fees.

## Web Sites

The following are some URLs for tax lien sale information for other counties in Colorado:

ADAMS: http://www.co.adams.co.us/index.cfm?d=home

ADAMS HAS INTERNET TAX LIEN AUCTIONS: http://www.co.adams.co.us/index.cfm?d=standard&b=1&c=14&s=107&p=914

ALAMOSA: http://www.alamosacounty.org/depts/Treasurer/index.html

ARAPAHOE: http://www.co.arapahoe.co.us/Departments/TR/index.asp

BOULDER COUNTY: http://www.co.boulder.co.us/treas/index.htm

BROOMFIELD: http://www.broomfield.org/centralrecords/Treasurer.shtml

DENVER: http://www.denvergov.org/PropertyTaxInformation/TaxLienSaleInformation/tabid/425589/Default.aspx

EAGLE: http://www.eaglecounty.us/treasurer/taxSale.cfm?id=1325

FREMONT: http://www.fremontco.com/treasurer/

GRAND: http://www.co.grand.co.us/treasuer/TaxSale/TaxSale.html

GUNNISON: http://www.gunnisoncounty.org/treasurer_tax_lien_sales.html

LARIMER: http://www.co.larimer.co.us/treasurer

LOGAN: http://www.loganco.gov/treasurer/index.htm

MESA: http://treasurer.mesacounty.us/default.aspx

MONTEZUMA: http://www.co.montezuma.co.us/newsite/treasurerhome.html

PARK: http://www.parkco.us/treasurer.htm

RIO BLANCO: http://www.co.rio-blanco.co.us/treasurer/

RIO GRANDE: http://www.riograndecounty.org/depts/treasurer/index.html

SUMMIT: http://www.co.summit.co.us/Treasurer/index.htm

WASHINGTON: http://co.washington.co.us/Elected_Officials/treasurer.htm

WELD: http://www.co.weld.co.us/departments/treasurer/index.html

## FLORIDA

Florida pays a good rate of interest (18%) but makes it much harder than other states to get the property. If the tax lien is not paid off, rather than just issuing a deed (as Arizona does, for example), in Florida, the property is sold at auction. You can bid in your tax lien certificate, but you are competing against anyone else who wants to bid for the property.

### Time of Tax Lien Auction

Rules 12D-13.045

Tax lien certificates on properties with delinquent taxes are sold on or before June 1 of each year.

### Conduct of the Auction

FS § 197.432

Each county's tax collector will begin to sell the available tax certificates at the yearly auction. Certificates that are not sold will be bought by the county, which will get the maximum rate allowed, 18% per year, simple interest. You can buy these certificates from the county and get the automatic 18% highest rate, without bidding.

12D-13.045

The tax lien certificate is sold "to the person who will pay the tax, interest, costs, and charges and who will demand the lowest rate of interest, not in excess of 18% per year." Therefore, the bidding begins at 18% and goes down from there. The charges include the cost of advertising.

The bidding on interest rates is by fractions of one-quarter of 1%. Therefore, if a bidder offers 17½% interest, the next acceptable bid will be 17¼%.

As soon as you are the lowest bidder, you must pay the tax collector a "reasonable deposit" within 24 hours.

When the tax lien certificate has been prepared, the tax collector will notify you, by whatever means necessary, and you must then pay the tax collector the remainder of the money owed within 48 hours. If you do not pay on time, you will lose your deposit.

### Void Certificates

§§ 197.432, 197.443, 12D-13.057, 12D-13.066

A tax lien certificate is occasionally void, either because the taxes on the property had really been paid or because of some error in procedure or because of an inadequate description of the land. In such a case, your money will be refunded, and you will receive consolation interest of 8% per year simple interest from the county.

## Lost or Destroyed Certificates

If a tax lien certificate is lost or destroyed, an application for a duplicate, accompanied by your affidavit, can be made to the tax collector. The fee for a duplicate is $5.

§ 197.433

## Transfer of Certificates

A Florida tax lien certificate can be transferred by endorsement at any time before it is redeemed or until a tax deed is issued after foreclosure. However, before the transfer is recognized and the transferee is paid any proceeds, the holder of the certificate must send the certificate in, along with a request for transfer. The charge for this service is $2.25.

§§ 197.462, 12D-13.054

## Buying Certificates Not Sold at Auction

Certificates not sold at public auction are issued to the county, where they accrue 18% interest until paid. Individuals can then buy certificates from the county.

If the tax deed application was made by the county and there are no other bidders, the clerk shall enter the land on a "List of Lands Available for Taxes." The county then has 90 days from the date of the auction to purchase the land for the opening bid. After 90 days, any person or government unit may purchase the land for the opening bid. Taxes will not be levied against parcels contained on the list but will be added to the minimum bid as they become due. If not purchased, lands contained on the list with any certificates issued on them on or before July 1, 1999, shall escheat (revert) to the county seven years after the date on which the property was offered for Tax Deed Auction. Unpurchased lands escheat to the county three years after the date on which the property was offered for Tax Deed Auction.

12D-13.064

## Payment of Lienholder on Redemption

A tax lien certificate can be redeemed at any time before the property is foreclosed on and sold for taxes. Anyone, including a mortgage holder, may pay the redemption costs.

If the property owner redeems the certificates, he must pay, in addition to the face amount of the certificate, any accrued interest, costs, and charges. One bonus is that even if the redemption is prompt, the property owner must still pay you a minimum of 5% interest to redeem the certificate.

§ 197.472

The tax collector shall receive a fee of $6.25 for each tax certificate purchased or redeemed.

## Application for a Tax Deed

§§ 197.502, 197.542, 12D-13.060, 12D-13.062-065

A tax deed is a deed to a property issued by the government. It wipes out the title of the former owner and the interest of his mortgage holder. In Florida, you will receive a tax deed only if you are the successful bidder at the tax sale.

Any time after two years have elapsed since April 1 of the year you were issued your tax lien certificate, you can file the certificate along with $75 and an application for a tax deed.

Although you can do this after two years, you do not want to wait seven years, because if you have not taken action by that time, the certificate expires and becomes worthless.

When you apply for a tax deed, you must be prepared to pay in more than just your tax lien certificate. You must also pay all other taxes owed on the property and the amount required to redeem all other tax certificates on the property, including interest and penalties. Finally, you will need to pay for a title search.

If the property is homesteaded, you will also have to pay one-half of the appraised value of the property.

## The Tax Sale

After the application and the required charges are received, the tax collector delivers the application and his certification to the local circuit court. The tax sale is advertised for four consecutive weeks, and notice is sent to various people including the property owner and any mortgage holder on the property. The sale cannot be held until 30 days after the first publications.

The successful bidder must pay for the property within 24 hours, usually by cash, a cashier's check, a bank draft, or a money order. If you did not buy the property, you will be paid the value of your certificate, plus the amount of your application, and additional interest of 18% per year from the time of your application, even if your certificate bore a lower rate of interest.

## Issuance of the Tax Deed

§§ 197.573, 197.662

The sale process ends with the issuance of a tax deed. Although this deed extinguishes the interest of the former owner and his mortgage holder, restrictive covenants running with the land are not extinguished. Occasionally, these can be bothersome, so it is worthwhile knowing the state of the title.

Assuming that the former owner has not vacated the property, you can apply to the circuit court for a writ of assistance to evict the former owner.

## Challenges to a Tax Deed

After the sale, the former owner may challenge the sale on a variety of grounds, including assertions that the procedures were not proper or that the taxes had been paid. You may bring a suit to quiet title or foreclose in order to head off any such challenges.

§§ 65.081, 197.602, 95.191

If it turns out that the sale was invalid for some reason other than prior payment of taxes, the sale will be canceled, but then you must be paid 12% per year from the date of issuance of the deed and all legal expenses in obtaining the deed. In addition, you must be paid the fair cash value of all permanent improvements you made to the property.

If you decide to go into "actual possession" of the property, then a four-year statute of limitations is triggered for anyone challenging your title under the deed. You have the same four years to bring an action against anyone other than the former owner in "adverse possession" (i.e., squatting) on the land.

## Local Procedures

As in other states, each county has variations of procedure. The following is the announcement by Dade County, Florida (where Miami is located), for its annual sale of tax lien certificates:

# DADE COUNTY, FLORIDA
**Dade County Tax Collector**
**Downtown Miami**
**140 W. Flagler St.**
**1st Floor**
**Miami, FL 33130**
**305-375-5452**
**http://www.miamidade.gov/taxcollector/home.asp**

The Tax Certificate Sale is conducted online as an Internet auction. The Web address for the sale is www. BidMiamiDade.com. Bidders will be able to view the parcels and begin submitting bids once the advertised lists of delinquent taxes are published in the Miami Daily Business Review that is scheduled for May 3, ____.

The Miami-Dade County Tax Certificate Sale begins on June 1, ____ at 8:00 a.m. EDT. Thereafter, the tax sale will begin each business day until all tax certificates have been offered for sale. Certificates will be sold individually and will be divided in batches of approximately 1,000 to 2,000 available for sale each hour. Batches will close each hour from 9:00 a.m. EDT to 5:00 p.m. EDT.

Public access for computers to access the sale will be at the South Dade Government Center, 2nd Floor Conference Room, 10710 Southwest 211th Street, Miami, Florida. Bidders must call 305-375-1829 if they require the use of a computer.

## REGISTRATION

All prospective buyers must be registered and be assigned a buyer number before they can enter any bids. Buyer numbers are assigned after a prospective buyer completes the online registration process and IRS Form W-9 at www. BidMiamiDade.com. Bidders who have been assigned a buyer number for a prior year's sale will be assigned that same number provided all registration information including name and taxpayer identification number remain the same as in the County's existing records; if not, a different buyer number may be assigned. Only one bidder number may be assigned to each taxpayer identification number.

Foreign Buyers must have an international taxpayer identification number (ITIN) in order to bid. IRS Form W-7 must be completed and filed with the Internal Revenue Service in order to obtain an ITIN.

DEPOSIT REQUIREMENT

All bidders will be required to post a deposit prior to the sale that is equal to 10% of their intended purchases with a minimum deposit of five thousand dollars ($5,000.00) required. Deposits must be submitted electronically via Automated Clearinghouse (ACH) through www.BidMiamiDade.com. Bidders will be limited to purchasing no more than 10 times any deposit received by the Tax Collector. Bidders will be allowed to increase their deposits at any time prior to a batch closing by submitting an additional deposit authorization. Each distinct bidder number will be required to post a separate deposit. It is suggested that prospective bidders check with their financial institutions prior to registering as not all accounts allow for the electronic transfer of funds through ACH.

TRAINING

Training is available to all bidders in several formats prior to the sale. There is a self-demo and daily trial auctions on www.BidMiamiDade.com. A prospective bidder can send an e-mail to lienauction@grantstreet.com or call (800) 410-3445, extension 1, to schedule a guided phone demonstration. Prospective bidders needing access to computers may call the Miami-Dade County Tax Collector at (305) 375-1829 to schedule use of a computer for training and registration prior to the sale date.

BIDDING PROCEDURES

In order to facilitate the online sale process, Miami-Dade County will be grouping the tax sale into batches of approximately 1,000 to 2,000 certificates per batch. Each certificate in the batch will be sold individually and in sequential order as advertised. The batches will be set based on the publication of the advertised list of delinquent taxes. The batches will close hourly beginning at 9:00 a.m. EDT and continuing until 5:00 p.m. EDT each business day until all certificates are sold. After a batch is closed, no new or changed bids will be accepted on certificates contained within that batch. No certificates will be sold out of sequence.

Bidders will be able to begin entering their bids into the system for all certificates and all batches beginning the day that the advertised list of delinquent taxes is published in the newspaper, which is currently scheduled for May 3, ____.

Florida law provides for a maximum interest rate of 18% and a minimum of 0% (no interest). Bids for each parcel shall be accepted in even and in fractional increments of one-quarter percentage (¼%) points only. If you wish to bid on a parcel, you must enter your minimum acceptable rate into the input cell on the web site and click the "Submit" button PRIOR to the close of the batch that contains that parcel.

The tax certificate is a lien issued to the lowest bidder who will pay the delinquent tax including interest, cost of sale, advertising and tax collector's commission of 5%. The entered bid is the minimum interest rate the bidder is willing to accept on the certificate and not necessarily the bid at which the certificate will be awarded. For example if an entered bid is 4.5% and the next lowest bid is 5%, the certificate would be awarded to the bidder with the entered bid of 4.5% but at the winning rate of 4.75%. The bid entered on any certificate can be changed, and/or submitted bids can be withdrawn at any point until the batch containing the certificate is closed. Only bids that are in "Submitted" status at the time of the batch closing will be counted. Bidders will not be able to see competing bids.

BID CAREFULLY. BIDDER CANCELLATIONS WILL NOT BE ALLOWED OR ACCEPTED. ALL SALES ARE FINAL.

Immediately following the closing of each batch, bidders will be able to review the unofficial results of the sale and see the winning bid and bidder on each certificate contained within that batch.

## AWARD OF CERTIFICATES

After the online sale is completed, the Tax Collector will review the results and balance the sale, confirming all payments have been received and removing any parcels that may have been erroneously included in the sale. Once the results have been verified by the Tax Collector, a final list of certificates will be available at the website. Each winning bidder will receive an email when the list is available, and will be able to log back into the web site, review and print a copy of their purchased certificates. Upon conclusion of the Tax Certificate Sale, the Tax Collector will provide each bidder an Official List of Certificates awarded to them. The Official List will be signed by the Tax Collector and mailed to the bidders.

Bidders will be required to authorize payment in full electronically via ACH within forty-eight (48) hours after notification of the final results is sent. Failure to make payment as required by the Tax Collector will result in the canceling of certificates issued to the non-paying bidder and the offering of those certificates for sale at a subsequent re-auction sale.

## RETURNED OR CANCELED PAYMENTS

Electronic or ACH payments are conditional payments until honored by the maker's financial institution and must be available for immediate withdrawal. Miami-Dade County Administrative Order 4-86 and Section 68.065, Florida Statutes provides that payment shall be canceled and subject to a fee of five percent (5%) the amount of the returned or canceled payment. Returned or canceled payments may result in the revocation of bidding privileges during the sale and/or a cancellation of any certificates awarded.

## Web Sites

The following are URLs for tax lien sale information for some other counties in Florida:

BAKER: http://www.bakercountyfl.org/taxcollector/default.htm

BAY: http://tc.co.bay.fl.us/Default.aspx

BREVARD: http://www.brevardtaxcollector.com/index.html

BROWARD: http://www.broward.org/revenue/welcome.htm

CITRUS: http://www.tc.citrus.fl.us/index.htm

ESCAMBIA: http://www.escambiataxcollector.com

JACKSON: http://www.jacksoncountytaxcollector.com/Default.aspx

LAKE: http://www.laketax.com/

LEON: http://www.leontaxcollector.net/index.html

PALM BEACH: https://www.bidpbtc.com/main

POLK: http://www.polktaxsale.com/

PUTNAM: http://www.putnamtaxsale.com/

SEMINOLE: http://www.seminoletax.org/tax/taxsale.shtml

SUWANNEE: http://www.suwclerk.org/mambo/index.php?option=com_content&task=view&id=24&Itemid=61

WALTON: http://www.waltontaxcollector.com/

# GEORGIA

The procedure followed in Georgia illustrates the blending of procedures between states said to issue "tax lien certificates" and those that conduct "tax auctions," which I explained in chapter 1 ("What Are Tax Lien Certificates?"). Georgia is included here because a person redeeming the property must pay a 20% premium for the first year or fraction of a year, on any taxes paid after the sale, and any special assessment on the property. After the first year, the person redeeming the property must pay an additional 10% for each subsequent year or fraction of a year that has elapsed since the date of sale, plus costs to redeem.

This state also illustrates the wisdom of exercising the right to pay the subsequent years' taxes. In many states, the failure to pay these taxes would merely mean that there would be another holder of a tax lien certificate, and you would need to pay off that lienholder before foreclosing. In Georgia, should you fail to pay a subsequent year's taxes and also fail to promptly foreclose on the tax lien, the purchaser of a later lien may foreclose and wipe out your lien.

One of the best descriptions of state procedures was prepared by the office of the tax commissioner of Cobb County, Georgia, where Marietta is located. This is the description:

## INTRODUCTION

There are several actions required by law in preparation for auctioning property. Information folders are kept on these parcels including our title search, tax map and/or plat, various correspondences, and our Ex-Officio Sheriff's Notice of Service. Our title searches are for our own purposes and would not serve the needs of the buying public. Keep in mind that it is the purchaser's responsibility to assure oneself as to the soundness of the title of all property sold at a tax sale.

Questions may arise that we cannot answer; therefore, the person interested in the property must find these answers in other offices and records. For example, we do not know building code requirements. We do not know whether county sewer lines serve any particular area or street. We have no way of knowing whether a particular parcel or lot will be approved for a building or a septic tank. We are not always aware of easements.

An important point that MUST NOT BE OVERLOOKED by the purchaser at a tax sale is that OTHER TAXES might be unpaid. If the parcel of land is located in a city that collects its own taxes, the city taxes could be unpaid as well. It is also possible that additional county taxes have become delinquent since proceedings first began on the parcel you are considering.

Can you lose money? Maybe! We don't really know. One can obtain a bad deed or title at a sale, whether from an individual or from a tax sale. We always recommend that anyone contemplating purchasing at a tax sale consult an attorney, assure oneself that the title is good, verify the information we have gathered, read those sections of Georgia law pertaining to tax sales and attend our sales to be familiar with the proceedings.

The buyer at a tax auction is responsible for proper processing of documents concerning the foreclosure of the owner's right to redeem and those documents concerning the right of redemption. Our office prepares and records the Tax Deed and the Real Estate Transfer Tax form after the sale.

## TAX SALE PROCEDURES

The Cobb County Tax Commissioner's Office follows certain procedures when it levies upon a piece of property. These procedures are prescribed by the Official Code of Georgia Annotated (OCGA). You will see code sections referenced throughout this booklet. These references are a starting point for your research and are by no means a complete listing. We strongly suggest you read those sections of Georgia law which pertain to Tax Executions and Tax Sales. OCGA Title 48—Revenue and Taxation, Chapter 3—Tax Executions, and Chapter 4—Tax Sales contain important information that you must be aware of. Also read and research those Opinions of the Attorney General and Judicial Decisions shown after each code section. These opinions and court cases are extremely important and must be taken into consideration when interpreting these laws.

FIERI FACIAS (FI.FA.)

A fi.fa. (short for fieri facias—a Latin term for "cause it to be done" and also used interchangeably with TAX EXECUTION or EXECUTION) is a tax lien or writ, authorizing the Sheriff or Ex-Officio Sheriff to obtain satisfaction of unpaid taxes by levying on and selling the delinquent taxpayer's property. These documents are recorded on the General Execution Docket (GED) of the Clerk of Superior Court. (OCGA 48-3-1 and 48-3-3)

AUTHORITY TO SELL

The Tax Commissioner of Cobb County also serves as Ex-Officio Sheriff of Cobb County. As Ex-Officio Sheriff, he appoints Ex-Officio Deputy Sheriffs to act in his behalf in tax sale matters. Each Ex-Officio Deputy Sheriff has full power to advertise and bring property to sale for the purpose of collecting taxes due the state and county. (OCGA 48-2-55)

Taxes due the state and county are not only against the owner BUT also against the property regardless of judgments, mortgages, sales, or encumbrances. Taxes constitute a general lien upon all property of a taxpayer and the lien attaches on January 1st of each tax year, even though a fi.fa. has not been issued. (OCGA 48-2-56 and 48-5-28)

30-DAY NOTICE BEFORE ISSUING FI.FA.

After the last day for payment of taxes, the Tax Commissioner notifies the taxpayer in writing that the taxes are outstanding, and unless taxes are paid within thirty (30) days, an execution (fi.fa.) will be issued. (OCGA 48-3-3)

ISSUANCE AND RECORDATION OF FI.FA.

At any time after the 30-day notice has elapsed, the Tax Commissioner shall issue an execution (fi.fa. or tax lien) against the owner and the property. The execution (fi.fa.) is directed "to all and singular sheriffs of this state" (which means Sheriffs or Tax Commissioners who serve as Ex-Officio Sheriffs) and shall direct them to seize and sell the property of the delinquent taxpayer to satisfy the delinquent taxes. The property shall be plainly described on the execution (fi.fa.). The execution also bears interest at the rate of 1% per month from the date the tax was due. The execution (fi.fa.) is signed by the Tax Commissioner as Ex-Officio Sheriff or may be signed by the Sheriff in a county where the Tax Commissioner does not serve as Ex-Officio Sheriff. The execution (fi.fa.) is recorded on the General Execution Docket (GED) of the Clerk of Superior Court.

LEVY

When real estate is levied, the levy officer who acts as an Ex-Officio Deputy Sheriff is directed by a tax execution to seize and sell the property to satisfy the delinquent taxes. The Ex-Officio Deputy Sheriff must give 20 days written notice before advertising to the owner, tenant, holder of the security deed, IRS, Georgia Department of Revenue and Labor and EPD or EPA (if outstanding federal tax liens or state of Georgia liens, EPD or EPA liens exist). The levy notice is delivered by certified mail, and if we cannot effect service by certified mail (mail returned unclaimed or undeliverable), the notice is delivered to the owner and/or tenant in person. The levy shall state the owner's and/or mortgage holder's name, the tax years delinquent, the principal amount of taxes due, the accrued cost due, and a description of the property to be sold. (OCGA 48-2-55, 48-3-1, 48-3-6, 48-3-9, 48-3-10, 48-4-3, 48-5-27, 48-5-161, 9-13-13)

POINTING OUT PRIVILEGE

If the property being levied upon is a house and lot, then the Tax Commissioner routinely seizes it all. However, if a large parcel (tract) is being levied, it may not be prudent to sell all of it, and a portion may be set aside for levy purposes. The delinquent taxpayer may select the property to be sold. This is known as the "pointing out privilege." However, it is at the discretion of the Ex-Officio Deputy Sheriff to levy on additional property whenever it is deemed necessary to secure prompt collection of delinquent taxes. (OCGA 48-3-4)

ADVERTISEMENT

All properties to be auctioned for delinquent taxes are advertised for four (4) consecutive weeks prior to the first Tuesday of the month. These advertisements are placed in the legal section of the Marietta Daily Journal under the heading "Tax Commissioner." Their website is www. mdjonline.com.—To view advertisements online, at the left margin click on, CLASSIFIEDS and from the drop down select, LEGALS and then to the right select, TAX COMMIS-SIONERS. These advertisements can be viewed online in the Friday edition! Each advertisement shows the owner's name, a description of the property to be sold, and the amount of tax due. (OCGA 9-13-140, 9-13-141, 9-13-142 and 48-2-55)

10 DAY NOTICE TO OWNER

A written notice is sent by certified mail 10 days before the tax sale to the owner address of record and any applicable state, county or municipality that has issued executions informing of the impending tax sale. (OCGA 48-4-1)

STARTING BIDS LIST

At noon on Friday before the auction, a final list of properties for sale and the starting bid prices will be available in the Levy Department.

TAX SALE

Our tax sale is held on the first Tuesday of each month, between the hours of 10 a.m. and 4 p.m., on the steps of the Superior Court building (except when the first Tuesday of the month falls on a legal holiday, the sale is held the next day, Wednesday). The opening bid for a particular property is the amount of tax due, plus penalties, interest, fi.fa. (lien) cost, levy cost, administrative levy fee, certified mail cost, advertising cost, and tax deed recording fees. The property is sold to the highest bidder. If no one bids, the Tax Commissioner has the authority to bid the property for the County. Properties receiving no bids may be offered for sale again at 3:00 p.m. on the sale date, if there are interested bidders.

PAYMENT

We require payment in full upon conclusion of the tax sale. Payment must be in the form of cash, certified check, cashiers check, or money order. We also require the purchaser to sign a statement attesting to the fact that the property was purchased for the final bid price.

Immediately following the conclusion of the tax sale all purchasers must remit full payment to this office. After all payments are processed we begin preparation of the Tax Deed and the Real Estate Transfer Tax form. These documents are normally recorded and mailed to the purchaser by Friday afternoon following the tax sale.

ACCORDING TO OCGA 9-13-170, ANY PERSON WHO BECOMES THE PURCHASER OF ANY REAL OR PERSONAL PROPERTY AT ANY SALE MADE AT PUBLIC OUTCRY WHO FAILS OR REFUSES TO COMPLY WITH THE TERMS OF THE SALE WHEN REQUESTED TO DO SO, SHALL BE LIABLE FOR THE AMOUNT OF THE PURCHASE MONEY. IT SHALL BE THE TAX COMMISSIONER'S OPTION EITHER TO PROCEED AGAINST THE PURCHASER FOR THE FULL AMOUNT OF THE PURCHASE MONEY OR TO RESELL THE REAL OR PERSONAL PROPERTY AND THEN PROCEED AGAINST THE FIRST PURCHASER FOR ANY DEFICIENCY ARISING FROM THE SALE.

SALE CLOSING

After the tax sale, we send written notice to the tenant, owner, security lien holder, IRS and the Georgia Department of Revenue and Labor (if applicable) informing them the property was sold. We provide them the purchaser's name and address. (OCGA 9-13-160, 9-13-161, 9-13-166, 48-2-55, 48-4-1, 48-4-3, 48-4-4, 48-4-6 and 48-4-20)

## AFTER THE TAX SALE

PAYMENT OF EXCESS FUNDS

After paying taxes, cost and all expenses of the sale, a letter is mailed to inform all parties of record that excess is available and to explain how to claim them. The funds will be distributed as the priority of interest exists. (OCGA 48-4-5)

If the potential exists for competing claims or when deemed necessary, we may file an interpleader action in Superior Court for the determination as to who is entitled to receive the funds. The funds will then be distributed to the parties according to the court order.

The letter and affidavit is mailed to the owner(s) of record at the time of the tax sale, each security lien holder(s) and to all other parties having any recorded interest. The affidavit is provided and used as a guideline for our record to disburse the funds.

The legal owner of the property, absent other lien holders, can claim the excess funds with an affidavit and indemnification agreement supported by a current Certificate of Title. Owners with one or more liens on the property may require the lien holder to release his interest in the funds in order for us to approve their claim.

The superior lien holder may claim the funds in the same manner. These claims should state the dollar amount of the lien on the property since the excess funds paid to the superior lien holder cannot exceed that amount.

## PROCEDURES FOR TAX PURCHASER, OWNER, CREDITOR AND PARTIES WITH RECORD INTEREST

### RIGHT OF REDEMPTION AND THE AMOUNT PAYABLE FOR REDEMPTION

When real property is sold at a tax sale the owner, creditor, or any person having an interest in the property may redeem the property from the holder of the tax deed.

The owner, creditor, or any other person with interest in the property may redeem the property at any time during the twelve (12) months following the tax sale. The purchaser of the tax deed cannot take actual possession of the property during this time. The tax deed purchaser is not authorized to receive rents or make improvements to any structure on the property or grade any lot prior to this time.

The redemption amount paid to the tax deed purchaser should include the amount paid at tax sale, plus a 20% premium for the first year or fraction of a year, any taxes paid after the sale and any special assessment on the property. After the first year, the purchaser is entitled to an additional 10% for each subsequent year or fraction of a year that has elapsed since the date of sale, plus costs to redeem. A premium of 20% is paid each year when the parcel is bid into the county. (OCGA 48-4-42)

When the property has been redeemed (all monies paid as prescribed by law), the purchaser shall then issue a quitclaim deed to the owner of the property (as stated on the fi.fa.) releasing the property from the tax deed.

When property is redeemed the quitclaim deed prepared by the purchaser shall include a recital indicating the name of the person who paid the redemption money and the capacity in which or the claim of right or interest to which the money was paid. The quitclaim deed shall be presented when payment is received or within 7 days from the date of the payment. The deed must be recorded in the county of the tax sale and the purchaser shall pay the recording cost and return the recorded deed to the redeemer. (OCGA 48-4-44)

The redemption of the property shall put the title conveyed by the tax sale back to the owner, subject to all liens that existed at the time of the tax sale. If the redemption was made by any creditor of the owner or by any person having any interest in the property, the amount expended by the creditor or the person interested shall constitute a first lien on the property. (OCGA 48-4-21, 48-4-40, 48-4-41, 48-4-42, 48-4-43 and 48-4-44)

## NOTICE OF FORECLOSURE OF RIGHT TO REDEEM

After twelve (12) months from the date of the tax sale, the purchaser at the tax sale may terminate or foreclose (bar) the owner's right to redeem the property by causing a notice or notices of foreclosure to be served by certified mail to the owner of record and to all interest holders which appear on the public record. In addition, the notice of foreclosure is to be published in the county in which the property is located, once a week for four (4) consecutive weeks.

If the redemption is not made until after the notice has been given, then the costs of serving the notice or notices and publishing the notice shall be added to the redemption price to cover the cost of making the necessary examinations to determine the persons upon whom notice should be served. (OCGA 48-4-42, 48-4-45 and 48-4-46)

Any questions about this foreclosure process should be referred to an attorney.

## AFTER THE RIGHT OF REDEMPTION IS FORECLOSED

After foreclosing the right of redemption, we recommend that the purchaser seek legal advice regarding the petition to quiet title in land pursuant to OCGA 23-3-60.

Under the action, the petitioner (tax deed purchaser) makes a request to the court to take jurisdiction over the matter. The court then appoints a Special Master (third party) to examine the petition and exhibits to determine who is entitled to notice. The petitioner will then ask the court to issue a decree establishing his/her title in the land against "all the world" and that all "clouds to petitioner's title to the land be removed" and that "said decree be recorded as provided by law."

## RIPENING OF THE TAX DEED TITLE BY PRESCRIPTION

AN ALTERNATIVE METHOD

The term prescription refers to a process whereby over a period of time a tax deed becomes a fee simple title. This process promotes an alternative method to obtain fee simple title without the legal intricacies of the foreclosure process.

A title under a tax deed properly executed at a valid and legal sale prior to July 1, 1989, shall ripen by prescription after a period of seven (7) years from the date of execution of that deed. (OCGA 48-4-48)

A title under a tax deed executed on or after July 1, 1989, but before July 1, 1996, shall ripen by prescription after a period of four (4) years from the execution of that deed. (OCGA 48-4-48)

A title under a tax deed properly executed on or after July 1, 1996, at a valid and legal sale shall ripen by prescription after a period of four (4) years from the recordation of that deed in the land records in the county in which said land is located. (OCGA 48-4-48)

Notice of foreclosure of the right to redeem is not required in order for the title to ripen by prescription. In order to protect your tax sale investment, subsequent taxes should be paid.

SUBSEQUENT TAX SALES

Until the right of redemption has been foreclosed or the title has ripened by prescription, a tax deed has the same force and effect as a lien. Since defeasible title has been conveyed to the tax deed purchaser, liability for subsequent taxes would be the same as any other superior lien holder.

If there is a subsequent tax sale of the same parcel, the tax deed purchaser will be listed as the owner along with the defendant in fi.fa. (record owner) for purposes of levy and sale, despite not having foreclosed the right of redemption or having the tax deed ripen by prescription. Therefore, the tax deed purchaser may wish to consider the best possible avenue to protect their initial tax sale investment.

Even though the tax deed purchaser may receive tax bills for subsequent taxes, the owner of record will continue to be the defendant in fi.fa. If and when the tax deed purchaser forecloses the right to redeem or the tax deed ripens by prescription and the tax deed purchaser takes possession, the tax deed purchaser becomes the record owner.

## Web Sites

The following are some URLs for tax lien sale information for other counties in Georgia:

AUGUSTA-RICHMOND: http://www.augustaga.gov/departments/tco/home.asp

BULLOCH: http://www.bullochtaxcommissioner.com/

CHEROKEE: http://www.cherokeega.com/ccweb/departments/tax/

DEKALB: https://dklbweb.dekalbga.org/taxcommissioner/index.asp?pg=TaxSaleGeneralInformation

FULTON: http://www.fultoncountytaxes.org/fultoniwr/01_depts_tax_comm.asp

GWINNETT: https://ssl.gwinnetttaxcommissioner.com/Property/information/TaxLienSale.aspx

HABERSHAM: http://www.habershamga.com/taxcommissioner.cfm

PEACH: http://www.peachcounty.net/taxes_delinquent.cfm

# ILLINOIS

The process of selling tax liens is different in two respects in Illinois: First, the state has two parallel systems with different rates of interest and different procedures. The "regular system" pays a decent 18%. However, the other system, under the "Scavenger Act," pays an even more impressive 24% interest per year. Second, the courts are more involved in the process of selling the liens than they are in other states. For example, the tax collector must bring the lien before the court before it can be sold. This gives more assurance to the buyer that the lien will be immune from attack later. On the other hand, you are more likely to need a lawyer in this state to get you through the process.

## Sale of the Liens

THE "REGULAR SYSTEM": After June 1 and September 1 of each year, if a property is delinquent, the tax collector will advertise a notice that he will apply for a judgment from the court allowing the sale of the property. The advertisement must be published at least 10 days before the application is made. It will list the lots, the names of the owners, the amounts due, and the years for which they are due. The property owner is notified by registered or certified mail.

The judgment for sale usually is obtained in October. The collector shall also give notice of a date within five business days after the date of application on which all properties for the sale of which an order is made will be exposed to public sale, at a location in the county designated by the county collector, for the amount of taxes and cost due.

§ 21-220

In order to bid at the tax lien auction, you must register 10 days in advance, and in the larger counties, you must deposit a letter or credit or bond for 1½ times the amount of taxes and penalties due.

§ 21-215

The winning bid will be the one that accepts the lowest rate of interest on the tax lien to be paid by the property owner. The bidding starts at 18% and goes down from there.

## $10 Automation Fee

§ 21-245

The county collector in all counties may assess to the purchaser of property for delinquent taxes an automation fee of not more than $10 per parcel.

The fee shall be paid at the time of the purchase if the record-keeping system used for processing the delinquent property tax sales is automated or has been approved for automation by the county board. The fee shall be collected in the same manner as other fees or costs. Fees collected under this section shall be retained by the county treasurer in a fund designated as the Tax Sale Automation Fund. The fund shall be audited by the county auditor. The county board shall make expenditures from the fund to pay any costs related to the automation of property tax collections and delinquent property tax sales, including the cost of hardware, software, research and development, and personnel.

THE "SCAVENGER ACT": The "Scavenger Act" applies only if a property is at least two years delinquent. Sales under this act may not occur every year in a given county, but they are supposed to take place at least once every two years. In reality, it can be longer than that between sales.

§§ 21-145, 21-150, 21-260, 21-270

In order to bid at the Scavenger Sale, you must register five business days in advance and may be required to pay a registration fee of $50 to $100.

Under this system, you do not bid on the amount of interest you will accept; that is fixed. Rather, you bid on the amount you will pay for the property. As a practical matter, this might not make much difference because if you bid an amount for the property over the amount of delinquent taxes, and the property owner later pays off the taxes plus interest to you, the actual yield on your investment is lowered by the additional amount you bid. For example, if the amount of taxes due is $1,000, the property owner will have to pay $240 to redeem at the end of one year. If you had bid $1,100, you would only get $140 in interest.

The minimum bid on property is $250 or one-half of the amount of taxes owed if that is less than $500.

The successful bidder must immediately pay the minimum bid to the county collector. If your bid is for more than the minimum, you have until the next day to pay the rest. Do not neglect to pay. If you don't pay, you will forfeit your minimum bid of up to $250. As if this were not enough, a collection suit can be brought upon failure to pay.

§§ 21-240, 21-260

§§ 21-250, 21-265

If you are the successful bidder, you will get a Certificate of Purchase. Before you get it, however, you must certify that you are not the delinquent taxpayer and that you have not failed twice to complete a tax lien purchase.

The certificate you receive is assignable by endorsement.

## Redemption of Foreclosure

§§ 21-75, 21-260, 21-355

As in other states, the property owner can redeem the property by paying the amount of the back taxes plus interest, penalties, and costs. If the lien was sold at the regular sale, then the penalty you bid will increase by the same amount every six months. If the property was sold under the Scavenger Act, the interest you pay will be according to the following table:

| TIME SINCE THE SALE | AMOUNT OF INTEREST DUE |
| --- | --- |
| Less than 2 months | 3%/month or part thereof |
| 2–6 months | 12% |
| 6–12 months | 24% |
| 12–18 months | 36% |
| 18–24 months | 48% |
| After 24 months | 48% + 6%/year |

§ 21-350

The amount of time you must wait before foreclosing varies with the type of property. The usual period is two years. For residential property under six units, however, the redemption period is two and a half years. For seven or more units, the period is six months from the date of the sale if the taxes were overdue by two years. An abandoned property may be foreclosed earlier on petition.

§§ 22-5, 22-10, 22-15, 22-30, 22-85

Within 4 months and 15 days after the tax lien sale, you must give a notice to the county clerk, to be given to the property owner, of the sale. Within 10 days of receipt of this notice, the county clerk must mail, by certified or registered mail, a copy of the notice to the property owner. Within three to five months of the end of the redemption period, you must give notice of the coming expiration of the period. Then, unless you get an extension, you must petition for a deed and record it within one year of the expiration period. If you fail to do this, your certificate is void.

§ 22-70

The property you get will not be free of easements. So, for example, if the electric company has an easement for its line, you are still stuck with that.

## Web Sites

The following are some URLs for tax lien sale information for counties in Illinois:

COOK: http://www.cookcountytreasurer.com/default.aspx

DEKALB: http://www.dekalbcounty.org/Treasurer/treasurer. html

LAKE: http://www.co.lake.il.us/TREASURER/default.asp

MADISON: http://www.co.madison.il.us/Treasurer/Treasurer. shtml

MCLEAN: http://www.mcleancountyil.gov/Treasurer/County_ Treasurer.htm

SANGAMON: http://www.co.sangamon.il.us/Offices/treas/ treasrer.asp

STEPHENSON: http://www.co.stephenson.il.us/treasurer/

Here's a link to other counties that use the Real-Time Auction

MANAGEMENT SYSTEM: http://www.iltaxsale.com/rams/ index-4.html

# INDIANA

Indiana has a complex procedure, with fatal deadlines for notices at the end of the redemption period and the bringing of the required court action to get a deed. Should you get through this minefield, though, up to 25% interest awaits you.

## The Tax Lien Sale

After taxes are delinquent for 15 months, the county treasurer (or in Marion County, where Indianapolis is located, the Metropolitan Development Commission) notifies the county auditor, who maintains a list of delinquent properties.

§§ 24-2, 24-2.2, 24-3, 24-4 (6-1.1–24-4.1 has been repealed)

The county auditor will notify the owners of the time and place of the public auction. Notice of the sale is sent to requesting mortgage holders and displayed in a "public place of posting" for 21 days. The notice is also published once a week for three weeks.

Not later than 15 days before the advertised day of the sale, a court will examine the list of properties, and not later than three days before the sale, the court will enter a judgment, and the clerk will prepare and enter an order for the sale.

§ 22-4.7

§ 24-2     The sale takes place on or after August 1 and before November 1 of each year. It continues until all properties have been offered.

§§ 24-7, 24-8     The winning bidder must "immediately pay." Failure to pay results in a penalty of 25% of the amount of the bid. The county prosecuting attorney may sue to collect this money.

§ 24-7     If the bid was for more than the taxes due, the excess goes to a "tax sale surplus fund." If the property is redeemed, the tax lien buyer will get this excess back. If the property is not redeemed, the excess goes to the delinquent taxpayer if a verified claim is made within three years.

§ 24-9     Immediately after receiving payment, the county auditor issues a "certificate of sale" that indicates the amount paid and the date when the purchaser is entitled to request a deed.

## Assignment of the Certificate

§ 24-9     The certificate is assignable, but the assignment is invalid unless it is endorsed on the certificate and registered with the county auditor.

## Lost Certificates

§§ 25-3, 25-4.6     A lost certificate can be replaced, but the county auditor must determine that the certificate did exist.

## Pre-Redemption Notification by Buyer

Indiana's major innovation is a short redemption period, coupled with complex notification procedures. If you buy a tax lien certificate in Marion County (Indianapolis), the county auditor will take care of the most technical requirements. Because of the detailed and complex nature of these notices and the extreme consequences of failing to get them exactly right, outside this county you should consult with an attorney. At the least, these notices should be prepared with careful attention to notification dates. The summary here is only general as to the timing and content of the notices.

§§ 25-4, 25-4.5, 25-7     The redemption period is one year. Not later than three months and not more than nine months before the expiration of this period, the tax lien buyer must give notice of the sale, the redemption period expiration date, the date on which the tax buyer intends to petition for a deed, and the amount required to redeem. The notice must be sent by certified mail to any person with a "substantial property interest of public record." If the address of a person with an interest in the property is unknown, notice must be given by publication for three weeks. If this notice is not given, then the lien terminates six months after the expiration of the redemption period. Another notice must be given of intent to seek a court order of the issuance of the deed.

## Redemption of the Property

The percentage interest that a property owner must pay in order to redeem the property depends on how long after the sale of the tax lien certificate the redemption occurs.

§§ 25-2

If the redemption occurs in less than six months, the interest is 10%. If it occurs in more than six months but less than a year, the interest is 15%. If it occurs in more than a year, the interest is 25%. Special assessments and taxes for subsequent years bear 10% interest. Ten percent interest is paid on the amount in the surplus fund.

## Obtaining a Tax Deed

To get a tax deed, the tax lien buyer needs to give the required notice and file a verified petition in the same court that authorized the sale. The court must issue the deed within 61 days if all the requirements have been met.

§ 25-4.6

After a tax deed is obtained, a quiet title action can be brought to determine its validity.

§ 25-14

The following are some URLs for tax lien sale information for counties in Indiana:

ALLEN: http://www.co.allen.in.us/index.php?option=com_content&task=blogcategory&id=83&Itemid=264

HAMILTON: http://www.co.hamilton.in.us/services.asp?id=4024&entity=2090

LAPORTE: http://www.laportecounty.org/departments/treasurer/index.html

MARION: http://www.indygov.org/eGov/County/Treasurer/home.htm

TIPPECANOE: http://www.tippecanoe.in.gov/treasurer/

This company handles tax sales for about 70 Indiana counties (SRI INC., 8082 BASH, INDIANAPOLIS, IN 46250): http://www.sri-taxsale.com/handout.pdf

# IOWA

In an effort to boost the sale of its tax lien certificates, Iowa dramatically increased the rate of interest its certificates pay to 24% per year. In addition to high interest, the ability to foreclose on a property in a short 21 months also makes Iowa an attractive state to consider. However, in Iowa you bid according to the percentage of interest in the property you will accept, and the winner becomes a co-owner with the delinquent taxpayer. This virtually ensures interesting discussions and court proceedings after the foreclosure. Moreover, Iowa is not a state where you can buy tax lien certificates directly from the county treasurers. Rather, Iowa allows purchases only at its tax lien auctions. Finally, Iowa requires that foreclosure occur before the end of three years. Still, 24% is mighty impressive.

## When Taxes Are Delinquent

§§ 445.37, 445.39 (All references are to Title 24 of the 2007 Iowa Code)

Property tax payments are delinquent on October 1 and April 1, respectively. During this delinquency period, the property owner will owe interest of 1½% per month.

## Notice of Delinquency and Sale

§ 446.9

Before May 1, the county treasurer will serve on the delinquent property owner by first-class mail a notice containing the property description, the amount of taxes, interest, fees and costs owed, and a statement of the period allowed for redemption. This notice is published once in an official newspaper at least one week, but not more than three weeks, before the sale.

In addition to the notice to the property owner, the mortgage holder and others with interests in the property are notified.

§ 446.11

If for some reason service cannot be made, notice can instead be posted in the treasurer's office for two weeks.

## The Sale

§ 446.7

The tax sale occurs annually on the third Monday in June. At that time, "the county treasurer shall offer at public sale all parcels on which taxes are delinquent. The sale shall be for the total amount of taxes, interests, fees and costs due."

§ 446.16

The competition works like this: "The person who offers to pay the total amount due . . . for the smallest percentage of the parcel is the purchaser, and . . . the percentage thus designated shall give the person an undivided interest." In other words, if the property is foreclosed and the purchaser agreed to take less than a 100% interest in the property, he becomes a co-owner with the delinquent taxpayer.

Unlike states such as Florida and Arizona, where the competition is about interest rates, and unlike states such as Colorado, where the competition is about the amount that will be paid, in Iowa, the amount to be paid and the interest rate to be earned are never at issue.

On the same day that the county treasurer sells tax liens on recently delinquent properties, liens that were not previously bought at other sales will also be sold.　§ 446.18

The sale continues from day to day as long as there are bidders or until all the available liens have been offered for sale.　§ 446.17

The successful bidder is required to "immediately pay to the county treasurer the total amount bid. Upon failure to do so the parcel is again offered as if no such sale had been made."　§ 446.23

If there are still unsold parcels, the county treasurer can adjourn the sale for up to two months and try again. The notice of the new date will be posted in the treasurer's office. If these liens are still unsold, the sale can be adjourned repeatedly until they are sold.　§ 446.25

The buyer will get a certificate of purchase that describes the parcel and the amount due and that certifies payment.　§ 446.29

## Lost Certificates

If a certificate is lost, it can be replaced upon submission of an affidavit and payment of a small fee.　§ 446.30

## Assignment of Certificate

As in all other states, Iowa tax lien certificates are transferable "by endorsement and entry in the county system in the office of the county treasurer."　§ 446.31

## Redemption of Property

The property owner can redeem by paying the county treasurer "the amount for which the parcel was sold . . . and interest of two percent per month, counting each fraction of a month as an entire month."　§ 447.1

If the property owner redeems, the county treasurer issues a certificate of redemption.　§ 447.5

### Foreclosure of Lien

§ 447.9

One year and nine months after the sale (or nine months if a lien more than one year old was bought at the sale) the purchaser may serve the property owner and any person in possession of the property with a notice containing a description of the property, the date of sale, and the name of the purchaser, stating "that the right of redemption will expire and a deed for the parcel be made unless redemption is made within ninety days from the completed service of the notice."

The purchaser must also notify the mortgage holder, any lessor or seller under a contract of sale, and those with recorded interests. The city where the property is located must also be notified. Only people entitled to this notice are allowed to redeem the property.

§§ 446.13, 446.10

The costs of the notice, and the record search necessary to give it, are added to the amount required to redeem. Once this service is made, an affidavit stating that the service was made and stating the amount of costs required to make it is filed with the county treasurer. It is this filing that completes the service.

§§ 448.1

Immediately after the expiration of the 90-day period from completed service, the purchaser may return the certificate along with a $25 fee, and the county treasurer will issue a deed.

§ 448.3

Even after the recordation of a deed, restrictive covenants governing the use of the property will still be valid.

### Loss of the Lien Through Failure to Foreclose

§ 446.37

"After three years have elapsed from the time of any tax sale, or after one year has elapsed from the time of any tax sale under section 446.19B, and the holder of a certificate has not filed an affidavit of service of notice of expiration of right of redemption under section 447.12, the county treasurer shall cancel the sale from the county system."

### Problems with the Sale

§§ 445.61, 448.6, 448.10

If it turns out that the property owner owed no taxes at the time of the sale, the treasurer's deed is invalid. If this or other problems are the result of the county's mistake, the county will indemnify the purchaser.

§§ 447.7, 448.12

The statute of limitations for raising problems with the sale is three years. However, in the case of minors and "persons of unsound mind," the period of redemption is not up until one year after the disability is removed, or redemption may be made by the guardian or legal representative at any time before the delivery of the treasurer's deed.

The statute of limitations may be shortened by filing an affidavit that the deed was recorded. Those with a claim on the property will then have just 120 days to assert their interest in the parcel.

§ 448.15

## Local Procedures

The following is information issued by the Treasurer of Polk County (where Des Moines is located) for tax lien certificates:

### MARY MALONEY
**111 Court Avenue**
**Treasurer of Polk County**
**Des Moines, Iowa 50309-2298**
**Tax Division**
**(515) 286-3060**
**Fax: (515) 323-5202**

The Annual Tax Sale is held by the Polk County Treasurer on the third Monday in June. The tax sale will begin promptly at 7:30 a.m. and continue each succeeding day for as long as buyers are present or until every parcel has been offered for sale. The County Treasurer will then adjourn the sale to 10:00 a.m. according to certain dates determined by the treasurer.

ELECTRONIC DEVICES PROHIBITED
Cellular phones, pagers, tape recorders, camcorders, and other audible electronic devices are to be turned off during the sale. Cameras, camera cell phones, and other picture taking devices are not allowed in the sale room or lobby area of the tax sale. A violation by the use of electronic devices may result in the disqualification of the bidder.

Laptop or notebook computers are allowed only if they are operated from battery packs.

### Registering for the Tax Sale

The Treasurer's Office will stop accepting registrations for the Annual Tax Sale when the maximum number of available bidders has been reached, as determined by the tax sale random selection software program. Registrations will be accepted in the order received by the Treasurer's Office. The Treasurer's Office will time stamp registration forms upon receipt using the date/time machine located in the Tax Division of the Polk County Treasurer, Room 155.

If the Treasurer's Office determines that a bidder has failed to make payment for tax sale certificate(s) in any county in Iowa, the auctioneer may disqualify the bidder from the sale; all certificates purchased by the disqualified bidder during the sale may be canceled and re-offered to other properly registered bidders.

Polk County recognizes one "interested party" for each bidder name/number. The interested party is the individual or, if the bidder is a company, the company officer who signs the "Registration of Tax Sale Bidder or Assignee," "Direct Deposit," and "W-9" forms, and is authorized to bid at the tax sale. If the bidder is a company, the signature and title of the company officer is required on all forms.

An "authorized agent" is an individual, other than the interested party, who acts as an agent/personal representative for the interested party as a bidder at the tax sale. Each interested party is allowed to designate one authorized agent per bidder number.

Registration of Tax Sale Bidder or Assignee: The interested party must properly complete the following forms:

    a. "Registration of Tax Sale Bidder or Assignee"—The interested party must complete and sign a "Registration of Tax Sale Bidder or Assignee" form for each tax sale year using the official unabbreviated IRS name for the bidder name.

b. W-9—The interested party must complete and sign a "W-9" form if one is not currently on file in the Treasurer's Office or if the bidder information has changed. The official unabbreviated IRS bidder name must be entered on this form.

c. "Direct Deposit Authorization"—The interested party must complete and sign a "Direct Deposit Authorization" form if one is not currently on file in the Treasurer's Office or if the information has changed. The official unabbreviated IRS bidder must be entered on this form. A voided check on the authorized account must also be attached.

d. "Agent Authorization"—The interested party may designate one individual per bidder number as an authorized agent to bid on his/her behalf during the Annual Tax Sale and all associated adjourned tax sales. To register as an authorized agent to bid, the interested party must complete and sign the "Registration of Authorized Agent" form on the back side of the "Registration of Tax Sale Bidder or Assignee" form using the official unabbreviated IRS name for the bidder name. The fee for designating an authorized agent is $75.00 per bidder number. An employee of the Polk County Treasurer's Office will not notarize this form.

TO REGISTER EARLY FOR THE ANNUAL TAX SALE: Bidders must be registered by 5:00 p.m. on the Tuesday before the Annual Tax Sale to be eligible to bid in the first session of the tax sale beginning at 7:30 a.m. on the third Monday of the month.

IF NOT REGISTERING EARLY FOR THE ANNUAL TAX SALE: Treasurer's staff at the Polk County Convention Complex will accept registrations beginning at 6:30 a.m. on the first day of the tax sale and then at 7:30 a.m. for each succeeding day of the tax sale.

## Bidding at the Tax Sale

Parcels with delinquent taxes are offered for sale in numerical sequence by an item number within each taxing district, as reflected in the official tax sale publication.

The tax sale consists of two sessions: regular and public bidder real estate sale items will be offered during the first session, and regular and public bidder mobile home items will be offered during the second session.

Each item will be offered for sale to all bidders considered "active" by the auctioneer, beginning with an opening bid of 100% undivided interest. (Note: "Active" means the bidder has properly registered and the bidder number is available for selection by the random selection software program used by the auctioneer.) After the auctioneer announces the next item to be sold, active bidders may bid downward a percentage of undivided interest. The bid-down percentage will give the winning bidder an undivided interest in the property upon issuance of a treasurer's tax sale deed. A "bid-down" will range in whole percentage points from 99% to 1%.

A bidder may submit a mailed bid if he/she cannot attend in person. The bidder must send the following information to the Polk County Treasurer's Office before the Friday prior to the annual or adjourned tax sale for which the bidder is placing a bid:

a. List of the item(s) on which he/she is placing a bid.

b. The lowest percentage of undivided interest per item the bidder is willing to bid for the item(s) requested.

PURCHASING TAX SALE CERTIFICATES

Payment is required at the conclusion of the sale, or at the time a bidder leaves if before the conclusion of the sale. The amount collected will include all delinquent taxes and special assessments, interest, special assessment collection fees, rates or charges, service fees, and a fee of $20.00 for each certificate to be issued. Payment must be in U.S. funds and in the form of a personal check, business check, money order, or any form of guaranteed funds for the exact amount of the purchase. Failure to make payment at the end of the sale will result in those items being re-offered to other bidders present before the tax sale is adjourned.

If a tax sale buyer's check does not clear his/her bank account, i.e., non-sufficient funds, account closed etc., the buyer will have five business days following notification from the Treasurer to repay with guaranteed funds or the tax sale certificate (s) will be canceled. A $30 fee will be assessed for each check returned unpaid.

Please allow up to 15 business days to receive purchased certificate(s).

The tax sale certificate of purchase does not convey title to the certificate holder. The titleholder of record or other interested party retains the right to redeem within the statutory period, depending on the type of tax sale. If the tax sale remains unredeemed after the statutory period, the certificate holder may begin action to obtain a tax sale deed. It is the interested party's responsibility to verify that the tax sale certificates received are correct for the parcels purchased.

## NOTIFICATION TO TITLEHOLDER OF TAX SALE

For each parcel on which taxes were sold, the county treasurer shall mail notification to the current titleholder, according to the mailing address on file in the Treasurer's Office, of the sale of delinquent taxes on the property. The notice will be sent by regular mail within 15 days from the date of the annual tax sale or any adjourned tax sale.

## REIMBURSEMENT OF A TAX SALE REDEMPTION

A redeemed tax sale will include the following:
a. The original tax sale amount, including the $20.00 certificate fee paid by the buyer at the time of the sale.

b. Interest in the amount of 2% per month, beginning with the month of the sale to the month of redemption, calculated against the amount for which the item was sold, including the $20.00 certificate of purchase fee. Each fraction of a month will count as a whole month.

c. Subsequent tax payments paid and properly reported by the certificate holder as an addition to the sale, with interest in the amount of 2% per month, beginning with the month the subsequent payment is posted to the county system to the month of redemption. Each fraction of a month will count as a whole month.

d. Valid costs incurred by the certificate holder of record and posted to the county system for action taken toward obtaining a tax sale deed. Costs not posted to the county system before redemption shall not be collected by the County Treasurer.

The buyer is responsible for checking redemptions for which he/she holds the certificate of purchase to inquire if redemption funds are available for payment.

Upon surrender of the tax sale certificate for a redeemed tax sale, either in person or by mail, the Polk County Treasurer's Cash Management Division will directly deposit the redemption proceeds to the buyer's designated checking account. The reimbursement will not be processed before the first business day following the cashier-validated date of redemption, as shown on the county's system. The Treasurer will mail a copy of the redemption certificate reflecting the total amount of the redemption to the buyer. Buyers should retain the redemption certificate copy for income tax purposes. A Treasurer's check will not be issued for redemption proceeds.

If the original certificate of purchase has been lost or destroyed, a duplicate can be obtained from the Polk County Treasurer's Cash Management Division at a cost of $20.

In the event a buyer has been reimbursed for a redemption and the taxpayer's check does not clear the taxpayer's bank account, the buyer will be notified by the Cash Management Division and will be required to immediately return the redemption funds. The Cash Management Division will return the tax sale certificate to the buyer and cancel the redemption. The tax sale will be reinstated as of the original sale date. A subsequent redemption will be calculated from the original date of the sale to the date of repayment.

### PAYMENT OF SUBSEQUENT TAXES (SUB-LIST)

A certificate holder may pay subsequent delinquent tax and special assessments, including rates or charges, on the same parcel(s) on which s/he holds the tax sale certificate. The Treasurer's Office will accept payments for subsequent delinquent tax and special assessments beginning 14 days following the date from which an installment becomes delinquent. Only items delinquent in the current fiscal year or a prior year may be paid on a "sub-list." Special assessments, rates or charges due in future years cannot be paid until the fiscal year in which they become delinquent.

A certificate holder must request a Sub-list Report of delinquent tax from the Tax Division of the Treasurer's Office. A report will be printed and ready the following business day. All requests for Sub-list Reports must be received at least one day before the posting of the payment to allow adequate processing time. All sub-list payments must be in our office by noon on the last business day of the month to allow adequate processing time. After sub-list payment(s) have been received and applied by the Treasurer's Office, the Treasurer will not refund the payment if the tax sale certificate holder later decides that he/she did not want to pay the delinquent tax on a particular parcel.

### ASSIGNMENT OF A TAX SALE CERTIFICATE

The tax sale certificate of purchase is assignable by endorsement on the back of the certificate, payment by the assignee of a $100 assignment transaction fee, and submittal of the certificate to the County Treasurer for posting to the county's system. A certificate cannot be assigned to another buyer who has redemption rights, except when the assignment is to a municipality. The assignor may not assign a certificate of purchase to more than one assignee/ buyer number.

A tax sale certificate of purchase and/or a tax sale deed can be set aside if it is determined that the tax sale buyer or assignee was ineligible to purchase the tax sale certificate.

Upon Treasurer's Office receipt of the $100 assignment transaction fee and the endorsed certificate, the assignment will vest in the assignee all the rights and title of the assignor.

### "90 DAY NOTICE OF RIGHT OF REDEMPTION" AFFIDAVIT

Service is completed when the certificate holder files the "90 Day Notice of Right of Redemption" affidavit with the County Treasurer. The certificate holder is responsible for determining the status of a tax sale before serving the "Notice of Expiration of Right of Redemption" upon persons who have a recorded interest in the property.

### REGULAR TAX SALE:

A tax sale certificate holder may serve a "Notice of Expiration of Right of Redemption" after one year and nine months from the date of sale.

### PUBLIC BIDDER SALE:

A tax sale certificate holder may serve a "Notice of Expiration of Right of Redemption" after nine months from the date of sale.

If the certificate holder fails to file a "90 Day Notice of Right of Redemption" affidavit within three years from the date of the tax sale, the County Treasurer will cancel the tax sale. In this instance, the certificate holder is not entitled to a refund.

## TAX SALE DEED

To request a tax sale deed, return the certificate of purchase and remit the appropriate deed issuance fee and recording fee to the Polk County Treasurer's Office. Payment must be in the form of a personal check, business check, money order, or any form of guaranteed funds. The fee for obtaining a tax sale deed is $25.00 payable to the Polk County Treasurer. The recording fee is variable as determined at the time a deed is requested and payable to the Polk County Recorder. All fees must be paid prior to delivery of the tax sale deed to the certificate holder.

The certificate holder must complete action to obtain a tax sale deed within 90 calendar days after the redemption period expires. The County Treasurer is required by statute to cancel the certificate of purchase when the tax sale certificate holder fails to comply. If the County Treasurer cancels the tax sale, the tax sale certificate holder is not entitled to a refund.

## ERRONEOUS TAX SALE OR ASSIGNMENT

If it is determined that any item was erroneously sold, the certificate of purchase will be canceled. This includes web payments received the day of the sale and prior to a successful bid. The certificate holder will return the certificate of purchase and the Polk County Treasurer will reimburse the principal amount of the investment. The Treasurer will not pay interest.

If it is determined that a county-held certificate was erroneously assigned, the assignment will be canceled. The certificate holder will return the certificate of purchase, and the Polk County Treasurer will reimburse the total amount paid for the assignment. Interest from the assignment date to the date of cancellation of the assignment will not be paid.

## Web Sites

The following are some URLs for tax lien sale information for other counties in Iowa:

BLACKHAWK: http://www.co.black-hawk.ia.us/depts/treasurer.
html

CARROLL: http://www.co.carroll.ia.us/Treasurer/treasurer.htm

CLINTON: http://www.clintoncountyiowa.com/treasurer/
default.asp

DALLAS: http://www.co.dallas.ia.us/treasurer/treasurer.asp

DELAWARE: http://www.iowatreasurers.org/iscta/access/
countyService.do?ID=1&ParentPage=28

DICKINSON: http://www.co.dickinson.ia.us/Department/
treasurer.asp

DUBUQUE: http://www.dubuquecounty.org/Treasurer/
tabid/111/Default.aspx

EMMET: http://www.emmetcountyia.com/

FLOYD: http://www.floydcoia.org/departments/treasurer/
index.asp

HAMILTON: http://www.hamiltoncounty.org/

JOHNSON: http://www.johnson-county.com/treasurer/index.
shtml

MARSHALL: http://www.co.marshall.ia.us/departments/
treasurer/taxes

POLK: http://www.polkcountyiowa.gov/treasurer/

POTTAWATTAMIE: http://www.pottcounty.com/html/Treasurer_
Tax_Sale.asp

SCOTT: http://www.scottcountyiowa.com/treasurer/

SHELBY: http://www.shco.org/treasurer.htm

WOODBURY: http://www.woodburyiowa.com/departments/
treasurer/

# LOUISIANA

Louisiana, which is a "loner" in several areas, has two unusual features in its tax lien certificates. First, the buyer can ask a court for immediate possession of the property; second, the buyer will collect at least 5% in penalties no matter how soon the property is redeemed. Along with the underlying interest of 12%, tax liens in Louisiana pay a total of 17% for the first year.

The tax collector will notify property owners by mail of delinquent taxes on January 2 of each year. If notification cannot be made that way, notification will be published. Notification will also be given to mortgage holders. The sale will be advertised 20 days after this notice is completed.

§§ 2180, 2180.1, 2181 (Unless otherwise indicated, references are to Title 47, Louisiana Revised Statutes.)

The sale must be held before May 1, if possible. It is conducted any time between 8:00 a.m. and 8:00 p.m. The purchaser must pay in cash, cashier's check, certified check, money order, or wire transfer in legal tender money of the United States.

§§ 2181, 2181.1, 2182

Within 30 days after the sale, the tax collector notifies the owner of the property of the amount required to redeem and the period allowed for redemption.

§ 2180

## Redemption of the Property

The property owner can redeem until three years after the sale has been recorded.

§ 2183

The cost of redemption is set by the Louisiana Constitution, making it difficult to change in future years. That cost is a flat 5% penalty, no matter when the property is redeemed, plus 1% interest per month. Although the penalty portion of the return is a great advantage if redemption occurs early in the first year, it also means that the interest rate is only 12% during the second and third years.

§ 2183, LA Constitution, Art VII, Ch. 25 (1974)

Still, in Louisiana, the property owner probably will not wait for the second and third years because the buyer can go into court and get an order for immediate possession of the property.

§ 2185

If the property is redeemed, the purchaser must be paid not only the principal, interest, and penalty, but also the value of all improvements made to the property. In addition, the purchaser gets the cost of maintenance, repair, and demolition required to meet property standard ordinances.

§§ 2222, 2222.1

If the property is not redeemed, this "shall operate as a cancellation of all conventional and judicial mortgages."

§ 2183

Three years after recording the sale, the purchaser can bring a quiet title action to eliminate any contest as to the validity of the sale.

§ 2228

## Web Sites

The following are some URLs for tax lien sale information for parishes in Louisiana:

ASCENSION: http://www.ascensionsheriff.com/PageDisplay.
  asp?p1=1789

CADDO: http://www.caddosheriff.org/index.htm

DESOTO: http://www.desotoparish.net/gov/dpso/index.asp

EAST BATON ROUGE: http://www.ebrpa.org/taxsales.html

RAPIDES: http://www.rpso.org/web/tax.htm

ST. CHARLES: http://www.stcharlessheriff.org/taxcollect.html

ST. JOHN: http://www.stjohnsheriff.org/tax_sale.htm

# MARYLAND

This state has high interest rates and short periods of redemption. The latter feature biases the process toward those looking to acquire the property and tends to increase the price at the sale.

Maryland is also unique in that the state is extremely indulgent of local variations, even in simple procedural matters. You should therefore be especially aware of local practices.

§§ 14-808, 14-812, 14-813 (All citations are to the Annotated Notifications of Delinquent Property Code of Maryland.)

The various counties in Maryland have their own rules about how delinquent a property must be before it can be sold.

Notification of sale is made 30 days in advance by posting the property on the city's Web site and by publication in a newspaper (the number of times varies by county).

## Conduct of the Auction

§ 14-817

The property is sold at auction for at least the amount of taxes, interest, penalties, and expenses. "The lien for the taxes, interest, penalties and expenses passes to the purchaser." In Baltimore City, a vacant and abandoned building can be sold for less than this amount.

§§ 14-818, 14-820

No later than the day after the sale, the successful bidder must pay to the tax collector the full amount of taxes due on the property sold, together with interest and penalties on the taxes, expenses incurred in making the sale, and the high-bid premium, if any.

Soon after the sale, a certificate of sale will be issued.

## Rates of Interest

The rate of interest paid if the property is redeemed varies by county. Assuming that the county did not decide differently, for example, the rates would be 14% in Carroll County and 10% in Caroline County. The rate in Baltimore City is 18%.

§ 14-820

Unless the tax collector has received written notice of an assignment giving the name and address of the assignee, he is authorized to treat the original purchaser as the holder of the certificate of sale and to pay any redemption money to him.

§ 14-828

## Required Foreclosure

After six months from the date of sale, you may sue to foreclose on the certificate of sale. The property owner can redeem until the decree is filed. Foreclosure is required within two years in this state. However, if you bought a lien on a building in Baltimore City that is vacant, you must foreclose within three months.

§§ 14-833, 14-845

The judgment of foreclosure cannot be reopened, except for fraud, after one year.

## Web Sites

The following are some URLs for tax lien sale information for counties in Maryland:

ALLEGANY: http://www.gov.allconet.org/tax/General%20 Information%20-%20Tax%20Sale.doc

ANNE ARUNDEL: http://www.aacounty.org/Finance/TaxSale. cfm

BALTIMORE CITY: https://www.bidbaltimore.com/

BALTIMORE COUNTY: http://www.baltimorecountymd.gov/ Agencies/budfin/finance/tax_faqs/taxsalefaq.html

CAROLINE: http://www.msa.md.gov/msa/mdmanual/36loc/ caro/html/caroe.html

CARROLL: http://ccgovernment.carr.org/ccg/collect/tax-sale. pdf

CECIL: http://www.ccgov.org/dept_treasurer/TaxSale.cfm

CHARLES: http://www.charlescounty.org/treas/taxes/taxsale/ taxsaleinfo.pdf

DORCHESTER: http://docogonet.com/index.php?page=tax_sale

FREDERICK: http://www.co.frederick.md.us/index.asp?NID=69

GARRETT: http://www.garrettcounty.org/FinancialServices/ TaxCollection.aspx

HARFORD: http://www.harfordcountymd.gov/FAQ.
cfm?&QuestionID=208

HOWARD: http://www.howardcountymd.gov/DOF/DOF_
HomePage.htm

MONTGOMERY: http://www.montgomerycountymd.gov/apps/
taxliensale/index.ASP

QUEEN ANNE'S: http://www.qac.org/default.aspx?pageid=401
&template=3&toplevel=34

SAINT MARY'S: http://www.co.saint-marys.md.us/
countytreasurer/taxsale-realproperty.asp

WASHINGTON: http://www.washco-md.net/treasurer/sale.
shtm#1

WORCESTER: http://www.co.worcester.md.us/trs/taxsale.htm

# MASSACHUSETTS

§ 29 (All
references are to
Chap. 60, General
Laws of Mass.)

Massachusetts is serious about collecting its taxes. An old law,
obviously not enforced, reserves the right to throw a property
owner in jail if he even looks like he might not pay, even if the tax
isn't due yet.

Compared with this, a tax lien sale may appear positively fes-
tive. However, tax lien sales are rare in Massachusetts. For example,
Boston keeps all its liens—and all the penalties—to itself. Worcester recently had a big tax lien sale. It was the City's first since 1993.
But the treasurer and tax collector of the City of Fitchburg says they
are planning to have sales in the future. With the economy declin-
ing, it is likely that there will be more counties having tax lien sales.
Check with local treasurer's or tax collector's offices for news.

### The Tax Collector's Auction

§§ 1, 37,
40, 42, 79

Property taxes become a lien on property on January 1 in the
year of assessment. If they are not paid within 14 days of a notice to
pay, the property can then be advertised for sale.

A notice of the time and place of the sale is published at least
14 days before in a newspaper in the town (or in a newspaper in
the county, if there is no town newspaper). The notice will state
the amount owed and the names of all owners and heirs. In addition, the notice will be posted "in two or more convenient public
places."

At the sale, the property will be sold "for the amount of taxes and interest, if any, and necessary intervening charges, for the smallest undivided part of the land which will bring said amount, or the whole for said amount, if no person offers to take an undivided part."          §§ 43, 44

In other words, as in Iowa, the price and the interest rate are constant; the bidding is for what percentage of ownership the bidders will accept upon foreclosure.

The winning bidder must immediately deposit the amount that the tax collector "considers necessary to insure good faith in payment of the purchase money." If this amount is not deposited immediately, the sale is void.

If the entire amount of the bid is not paid within 20 days, the sale is likewise void, and the deposit is forfeited.          § 49

The winning bidder gets a "collector's deed." This deed does not grant possession of the property, but it is held as security for repayment until the right of redemption expires. The deed comes with a warranty that the sale was conducted according to law.          § 45

If there is no bidder at the auction, the treasurer of the city or town can sell the property at another auction.          § 48

### Recording the Deed

The winning bidder must be sure to record the deed promptly. The deed is invalid if not recorded within 60 days after the sale.          § 52

### Appointment of Local Representative

In an odd gambit, apparently to increase local employment, if the winning bidder does not reside in the town, he "shall appoint an agent residing therein . . . authorized to release such land." A resident can simply file with the treasurer and record a notice of his residential and business addresses.          § 47

### Redemption of Property

The property owner can redeem by paying the amount of the lien plus 16% per year interest and any charges that have attached.          §§ 62, 63

The money may be paid to the purchaser, to the purchaser's designated representative or assign, or to the treasurer. This procedure is unique to Massachusetts. In other states, no option is given to pay the lienholder directly; the money always goes to the local agency.

If the property owner pays the treasurer, the treasurer will then turn the money over to the purchaser.

The property owner need not pay the entire amount at once, however. Instead, he can pay in installments as long as the first installment is 25% of the total cost to redeem the property. During the term of the agreement, the treasurer may not bring an action to foreclose the tax title unless payments are not made in accordance with the schedule set out in the agreement. If the property owner elects this installment route, he is given an extra two years to pay the taxes without danger of foreclosure.

## Foreclosure of the Property

§ 64

If the tax lien is not repaid within six months, a petition can be brought in "land court" to foreclose on the property.

§§ 66,
67 68, 71

The court will notify interested people, including mortgage holders, of a hearing date at least 20 days after the notice. On or before that date, an interested person can offer to redeem "upon such terms as may be fixed by the court." In this state, a person redeeming is also liable for attorney's fees. A person contesting the foreclosure can demand a jury trial.

§ 69

If no appearance is made by a person offering to redeem or contesting the proceeding, the purchaser can make a motion for a default decree. This will "forever bar all rights of redemption" except that within one year (or within 90 days if the property is abandoned), the court can vacate the decree if the property has not been resold to an innocent purchaser.

§ 84A

If the tax sale is declared to be invalid, the treasurer will refund the amount paid plus interest at 6% for up to two years.

A state official warned that although the foreclosure action can be filed in six months, between backlogged courts and property owners requesting extensions, the matter may not be completed for up to three years.

## Web Sites

The following are some URLs for tax lien sale information for municipalities in Massachusetts. In addition, you can find all the numbers you need at http://www.masscta.com/members.php.
FITCHBURG: http://www.ci.fitchburg.ma.us/city_government.
htm. (It's better to ask questions by phone at (978) 345-9605 because the Web site isn't much help.)

HUDSON: http://www.townofhudson.org/Public_Documents/
  HudsonMA_Collector/collector
WORCESTER: http://www.ci.worcester.ma.us/trs/

# MISSISSIPPI

### The Land Tax Sale

In Mississippi, all taxes are due by February 1. But any county may, by an order of the board of supervisors, allow partial payments. If partial payments are allowed by the county or municipality, they shall be paid as follows: one-half by February 1, one-fourth by May 1, and one-fourth by July 1. After August 5 of each year, for two weeks, a list of delinquent properties will be published in a newspaper, along with the amounts owed. If no newspaper exists in the county, the list will be posted. In either case, the notice will announce a tax lien sale on the first Monday in April or the last Monday in August.

The sale will take place between 8:30 a.m. and 4:30 p.m. If a large parcel is for sale, the first 40 acres or a smaller subdivision will be sold first. If the buyer does not "immediately pay," he can be sued.

If the sale is for more than the amount owed, the excess is held by the county treasurer. If the property is redeemed, the amount is refunded to the tax lien buyer. If not, then the landowner gets this excess. If the owner of the property does not request payment of the excess within two years from the expiration of the period of redemption, the excess shall be retained by the county.

On or before the second Mondays in May and October, a list of sold properties goes to the clerk of the Chancery Court.

### Redemption of the Property

The property owner can redeem within two years from the sale. The redemption requires payment of 5% "damages on the amount of taxes for which the land was sold, and interest on all such taxes at the rate of one and one-half percent per month, or any fractional part thereof, from the date of such sale, and all costs that have accrued on the land since the sale."

This interest rate structure allows the buyer the greatest returns on early redemption. If the redemption occurs in one week, the

§§ 27-41-1, 27-41-55, 27-41-57, 27-41-59 (All references are to the Mississippi Code Annotated.)

§§ 27-41-59, 27-41-73

§§ 27-41-77, 27-41-79

§ 27-45-3

6½% (5% penalty plus 1½% interest) earned would annualize at a (purely theoretical) 338% per year. The interest rate is 18% (1.5% per month) per year, and the redemption period is two years.

The two-year limit for redemption is extended for minors and people of unsound mind who can redeem within two years of reaching adulthood or being restored to sanity, respectively. Although they can get their property back, they must pay the value of any improvements made after two years.

If a mortgage is secured by only part of the land sold, then the mortgage holder is permitted to redeem only that part.

### Obtaining a Tax Deed

§ 27-45-23

At the end of the two-year period, the chancery clerk will, on demand, execute a deed. The tax lien buyer will then get "a perfect title with the immediate right of possession."

§ 27-45-27

If the sale is invalidated for any reason, the buyer will still get a lien for the 5% penalty plus 18% per year interest.

### Web Sites

The following are some URLs for tax lien sale information for counties in Mississippi:

DESOTO: http://www.desotoms.com/tax_sale.htm

JACKSON: http://www.co.jackson.ms.us/DS/TaxCollector.html

LAMAR: http://www.lamarcounty.com/cms/index.php?
option=com_news_portal&Itemid=41

MADISON: http://www.madison-co.com/elected_offices/tax_
collector/index.php

PIKE: http://www.co.pike.ms.us/tax.html

# NEW HAMPSHIRE

A tax lien sale has become a rare event in New Hampshire, perhaps because its frugal counties and municipalities would rather keep the penalties than get the cash. Still, they are authorized by state law, and you might find one.

§§ 80:20a,
80:24 (All
references are to
New Hampshire
Revised Statutes
Annotated.)

### The Tax Lien Auction

Tax lien auctions may be held by both counties and cities or towns. The bidding is not based on the percentage return you will get or on how much you will pay; those are fixed. Rather, as in Iowa, "every such sale shall be at auction for the percentage of the common and undivided interest in the whole property that a bidder is willing to offer for the unpaid tax, interest and costs due thereon."

The tax collector gives notice of the sale by posting advertisements at two or more public places at least 25 days before the sale. Notice is also to be sent by registered mail to the delinquent taxpayer 30 days before the sale.        § 80:21

The sale will take place between 10:00 a.m. and 6:00 p.m. It can be adjourned for up to three days.        § 80:24

The tax collector sends information about the results of the sale to the registrar of deeds, who will record it.        § 80:27

## Notification of Mortgage Holder by Buyer        §§ 80:28, 80:29

New Hampshire has a unique procedure that can cause a real problem if ignored. Within 45 days of purchase, the tax lien buyer must notify mortgage holders, as determined by the county records, of the sale. This notice can be sent in person or by registered mail. Unless this is done, the tax sale is not valid as against the mortgage holder. Nevertheless, even if this notice is not given, the tax lien buyer can sue the taxpayer for the taxes paid.

The tax lien buyer may pay subsequent years' taxes. In such a case, the mortgage holder must be notified within 30 days of these payments. The subsequent payments also earn interest at the rate of 18%.        §§ 80:29, 80:37

## Redemption of the Property

The property may be redeemed by paying the tax collector the amount for which the property was sold, plus 18% interest. Partial redemption payments can be made in multiples of $5. Part owners may redeem only their shares if they wish.        §§ 80:30, 80:32, 80:35, 80:37, 80:69

## Issuance of Tax Deed

If the property is not redeemed within two years, the tax collector will send notification to the property owner by certified mail. After 30 days, if the property is still not redeemed, the tax collector will issue a deed to the tax certificate buyer.        §§ 80:38, 80:38a

There is a 10-year statute of limitations for contesting the validity of the tax sale and the tax deed.        § 80:39

# NEW JERSEY

Tax liens are sold in New Jersey not only by counties but by every agency that collects taxes. If you are thinking about investing in New Jersey tax lien certificates (called "certificates of purchase" in that state), be sure to review chapter 15 and heed its advice about avoiding environmental liabilities. True, New Jersey calls itself the "Garden State," and there is justification for the claim, as much of the state is lovely. At the same time, because of its boisterous and uncontrolled industrial history, New Jersey has more hazardous waste dump sites per square mile and more numerically than any place outside Eastern Europe.

New Jersey's tax lien certificates pay a healthy 18%, plus a penalty of 2–6%. However, its rules are more complex than those in most states. This summary omits some of the details.

## Notice of Tax Lien Sale

§§ 54:5-19, 54:5-21, 54:5-25 (All references are to Title 54, New Jersey Codes Annotated, known as the "Tax Sale Law.")

Taxes are delinquent on November 11 in the year they are due. The tax collector makes a list, current as of November 11, of these properties.

A public notice of the tax sale of these properties is given, which contains a description of the lots, the owners' names, and the amount of taxes due as of the date of the tax sale.

The notice of sale must be posted in "five of the most public places in the municipality." (In the Tax Sale Law, any taxing agency is called a "municipality.") In addition, a notice is published in the local newspaper for four weeks before the week of the sale. The notice is mailed to the property owner.

## Conduct of the Sale

§§ 54:5-31, 54:5-32, 54:5-33, 54:4-46

The sale is at auction for the amount advertised. "The sale shall be made in fee to such person as will purchase the property, subject to redemption at the lowest rate of interest, but in no case in excess of 18% per annum." If anyone is inclined, the bid can be at no interest and even a premium above the taxes. Payment for the sale shall be made before the conclusion of the sale. The successful bidder gets a certificate of sale.

§ 54:5-52

After two years, no attack, except on the ground of fraud, can be made on the validity of the certificate of sale.

## Recording the Certificate of Sale

Within three months of the date of sale, the buyer should re-cord the certificate of sale in the office of the clerk or registrar of deeds. The certificate is recorded as the equivalent of a mortgage.

§§ 54:5-50, 54:5-51

Unless this recording is made, the property owner can wipe out this certificate by selling the property to a "bona fide purchaser" (that is, one without notice of your lien) or leasing or mortgaging the property to others without notice of the lien.

## Redemption by Property Owner

The property owner can simply pay the taxes before the sale. If the sale goes forward, the property owner can redeem within 10 days of the sale by paying the amount you paid at the sale plus interest. After 10 days, the property owner who wants to redeem must also pay (if you give an affidavit) subsequent municipal liens that you have paid, plus a penalty of 2% if the cost to redeem is more than $200, 4% if it is more than $5,000, and 6% if the cost to redeem is more than $10,000.

§§ 54:5-29, 54:5-58, 54:2

This redemption can be made not only by the property owner but also by a "mortgagee, or occupant of land sold for municipal taxes."

§ 54:5-54

The right to redeem extends for two years from the date of sale when the purchaser is other than the municipality or at any time thereafter until the right to redeem is cut off.

If a redemption occurs, a certificate of redemption is issued, which may be recorded. If your certificate of sale is canceled, you will be notified and paid the redemption monies upon your return of the certificate of sale.

§§ 54:5-55, 54:5-57

## Foreclosing on the Lien

After a right to redeem expires, you will foreclose. Written notice is given to the property owner of his right to redeem. The notice will state that if no redemption occurs within two years after the date of sale, the right to redeem will be barred.

§§ 54:5-82, 54:5-114.4

The property owner must be sent a notice by mail at least five days before the taking of action by the governing body. In addition, notice shall be posted in three public places in the municipality at the same time the notice is mailed to the property owner. In mu-nicipalities having more than 5,000 inhabitants, the notice shall be published at least once in a public newspaper published or circu-lated in the municipality within five days before action is taken.

§ 54:5-79

If the property owner still does not redeem the property within the time given in the notice, the right to redeem is barred. On the other hand, if you do not foreclose within 20 years of the purchase, you are barred from foreclosing unless you paid all property taxes each year.

§§ 54:5-81, 54:5-82

The county clerk or registrar, as the case may be, shall index the notice, affidavits, and certificates in the alphabetical index of grantors in the name of the delinquent owner, as shown by the certificate, and in the name of every person who has been served with notice as an interested party, as shown by the affidavit, and shall note in the margin of the original record of the certificate in the books of mortgages a reference to the place where the certificate and affidavits have been re-recorded as a deed.

§§ 54:5-84, 54:5-97.1, 54:5-104.64(b), 54:104-67

After two years, and absent fraud, there can be no attack on the service of your notice or other irregularities, except by minors or people who are judged to be incompetent. If you want your title to be safe from minors or people who are judged to be incompetent, you need to foreclose in the superior court. To do this, you must give 30 days' notice of the intent to file a complaint and the amount due, or else you will not receive your filing fee and counsel fees if you sue. After you get your judgment of foreclosure and after three months, except on the grounds of lack of jurisdiction or fraud, there can be no application to reopen the judgment.

## Unsold Liens

§§ 54:5-112, 54:5-113

Liens that are not sold at the auction can be sold by the municipality at a private sale or at another auction for not less than the amount of the liens or, if the liens are for more than the assessed value, then for the assessed value. By resolution, the municipality can sell at a lower price.

A statute enacted in December 1993 allows one or more municipalities to package and sell tax lien certificates under the terms and conditions set forth in the resolution of the governing body.

§§ 54:5-113, 54:5-114.6

If you do buy from the municipality, pay careful attention to the rules, because special time limits apply to redemption and foreclosure, and if you miss your limit and have not gotten an extension of time to foreclose from the municipality, you will lose what you paid for the lien.

## Defective Liens

If the tax lien sale is voided, a lien for what you paid remains in effect.

Even if the sale was defective, the sale cannot be set aside unless the tax is paid, along with interest and charges.

When you buy at a defective tax sale and intend to occupy the property, special rules apply.

New Jersey is not as generous as some states, which will have the taxing agency pay you a certain rate of interest if the sale is void because of some fault of the agency.

§ 54:5-42

§ 54:5-43

§ 54:5-104.100

## Web Sites

The following are some URLs for tax lien sale information for townships in New Jersey:

ABERDEEN TOWNSHIP: http://www.aberdeennj.org/dept_tax_coll_main.html

CITY OF PLEASANTVILLE: http://www.pleasantville-nj.org/index.asp?var_incl=collector.lbi

DENVILLE TOWNSHIP: http://www.thedenvillehub.com/dept-finance-tax.asp

EASTAMPTON TOWNSHIP: http://eastampton.com/Main/Tax%20Collector.htm

FRANKLIN TOWNSHIP: http://www.franklintwpnj.org/dept_revenue_collection1.html

HAMILTON TOWNSHIP: http://hamiltonnj.com/government/finance_revenue.htm

HOPEWELL TOWNSHIP: http://www.hopewelltwp.org/tax_collector_main.html

LACEY TOWNSHIP: http://www.laceytownship.org/content/71/default.aspx

MENDHAM TOWNSHIP: http://mendhamtownship.org/finance.htm

MIDDLE TOWNSHIP: http://www.middletownship.com/tax/tax.htm#TaxSale

NORTH HANOVER TOWNSHIP: http://www.northhanover.us/subpages/taxation/taxOffice.html

OLD BRIDGE TOWNSHIP: http://www.oldbridge.com/content/50/140/178/default.aspx

PEMBERTON TOWNSHIP: http://www.pemberton-twp.com/tax_collector

WESTAMPTON TOWNSHIP: http://www.westampton.com/
   Administration/content/TaxCollector.asp
WEST MILFORD TOWNSHIP: http://www.westmilford.org/Cit-e-
   Access/FAQ/index.cfm?TID=11&DID=442#F250
WINSLOW TOWNSHIP: http://www.winslowtownship.com/
   content/131/default.aspx

# WYOMING

Wyoming is another state, like Iowa, where you do not bid the amount of interest you will get or even the amount of cash you will pay but, rather, the extent of the interest in the property you will accept. What you receive is a Certificate of Purchase of the property. This is just a fiction, though, because the owner has four years to redeem, after which you may apply for a Tax Deed.

## When Taxes Are Delinquent

§ 39-13-107 (All section references are to the Wyoming Statutes.)

One-half of the property tax is due on and after September 1 and payable on and after November 10 in each year, and the other half of the tax is due on and after March 1 and payable on and after May 10 of the succeeding calendar year. The tax is delinquent as of May 11. A list of delinquent taxes is prepared by May 21.

## Rate of Interest

§ 39-13-108

Delinquent taxes bear a rate of interest of 18% per year.

## Conduct of the Auction

§ 39-13-108

The auction of Certificates of Purchase is advertised once each week for three weeks in a legal newspaper. The first publication must be four weeks before the sale and conclude before the first week in September.

The auction is held at the county courthouse or county building between 9:00 a.m. and 5:00 p.m., except Sundays.

The Certificate of Purchase is sold to "any person who offers to pay the amount of taxes, interest, penalties and costs including charges . . . due on any real property."

The successful bidder must "immediately" pay the county treasurer. The buyer will get a Certificate of Purchase that is entered by number in the county rolls.

## Unsold Certificates

Any certificates that are not sold go to the county treasurer. The county may sell those certificates "at public or private sale at any time."

§ 39-13-108

## Assignment of Certificates

You may assign your Certificates of Purchase to another person by endorsing them.

§ 39-13-108

## Redemption by Property Owner

If the property is "sold" (that is, if a Certificate of Purchase is issued), the property owner may redeem the property within four years from the date of sale. If the property owner does redeem, he gets a Certificate of Redemption. The county treasurer will then notify you of the redemption.

§ 39-13-109

## Obtaining a Tax Deed

At least four years, but not more than six years, after you get your Certificate of Purchase, you may apply to the county treasurer for a Tax Deed.

§ 39-13-108

To do this, at least three months beforehand, you must have completed service of notice on each person in possession of the property and each person in whose name the property was taxed or assessed, as well as the mortgage holders. The service on the owners can be by publication if they cannot be served personally.

Service by publication requires that the notice be published once per week for three weeks, with the first publication occurring not more than five months before the application for the tax deed. You must also send a notice by certified or registered mail to the owners of record and the mortgage holders.

The notice must contain the following information:

(A) When you purchased the property (i.e., when you got your Certificate of Purchase)
(B) In whose name the property was taxed
(C) The legal description of the property
(D) The year the property was taxed or assessed
(E) When the time of redemption will expire
(F) When an application for a Tax Deed will be made
(G) The amount of any special assessments for local or public improvements

After the notification is complete and you have waited three months, you can return the Certificate of Purchase, pay the required fees, and prove your compliance with the notice provisions. Proof of service by publication requires the sworn statement of the newspaper's publisher, manager, or editor.

Once you have done all this, you will receive a Tax Deed. As holder of a Tax Deed, you are entitled to possess the property.

### If the Tax Deed Is Attacked

§ 39-13-108    Occasionally, a Certificate of Purchase or a Tax Deed is issued in error. For example, the property owner may have paid the tax, and the county forgot to record it.

If the sale is void because of a mistake by the county treasurer, the county will pay you what you would have received upon redemption.

If the sale is void for some other reason, you are given a lien carrying 8% interest. This lien is for your payments of taxes, costs, penalties, interest, and the value of improvements to the property that you have made.

§ 39-13-110    This lien is superior to all other liens, except those created by other tax sales or the payment of taxes by another person. You can foreclose on this lien and have the property sold. At the sale, you can bid in the amount of your lien.

The lien can be foreclosed between 4 and 10 years after the original purchase. If no taxes were ever due, however, you cannot foreclose but must look to the county to pay for its mistake.

### Web Sites

The following are some URLs and contact information for tax lien sale information for counties in Wyoming:

ALBANY: http://www.co.albany.wy.us/Departments/Treasurer/tabid/65/Default.aspx

BIGHORN: http://www.bighorncountywy.gov/dept.php?name=treasurer&namev=Treasurer

CONVERSE: http://www.conversecounty.org/gov_admin/treasurer/taxsale.html

FREMONT: http://fremontcountytreasurer.org/info/index.php

GOSHEN: http://goshencounty.org/Treasurer/Default.asp

LARAMIE: http://www.laramiecounty.com/_departments/_treasurer/index.asp

LINCOLN: http://www.lcwy.org/taxsale.asp
SHERIDAN: http://www.sheridancounty.com/treas/property_
   tax_guide.pdf
SWEETWATER: http://www.co.sweet.wy.us/treas/
   propertytaxes/index.html
TETON: http://www.tetonwyo.org/treas/
UINTA: http://www.uintacounty.com/index.asp?nid=24

**APPENDIX III**

# Environmental Forms for Commercial and Industrial Properties

As I discussed in chapter 15, one of the advantages of specializing your investments in residential properties is that they require far less investigation.

Nevertheless, because commercial and industrial properties may present very attractive opportunities, I have included two forms to get you started in checking out these properties.

The first of these forms is a "Pre-Audit Environmental Questionnaire," which poses some initial questions about the property and may reveal disqualifying problems immediately. The second form is a "Phase 1 Consultant Contract," which you can use to engage environmental professionals to assist you.

If you are drawn to investments in commercial and industrial properties, you should consider obtaining my book *Environmental Liability and Real Property Transactions* (Aspen Publishers), which contains several more useful forms, along with a complete treatment of environmental issues, updated each year.

# FORM 1

## Pre-Audit Environmental Questionnaire

1. FACILITY ADDRESS: _____

   _____

2. CONTACT AT FACILITY:

   Name: _____ Phone: _____

3. PROPERTY OWNER: _____

4. ZONING: _____

5. PROPERTY SIZE: _____

6. TENANTS:

   Company name _____ Building number _____

   Company name _____ Building number _____

   Company name _____ Building number _____

7. BUILDINGS:

   | Building number | Uses | Square feet | Age |
   |---|---|---|---|
   |  |  |  |  |
   |  |  |  |  |
   |  |  |  |  |

8. PREVIOUS USES OF SITE:

_____

_____

_____

9. ARE ANY UNDERGROUND TANKS CURRENTLY LOCATED AT THE FACILITY?

Yes _____    No _____

10. IF THE ANSWER TO #9 IS "YES," THEN FOR EACH TANK LIST:

Contents        Age        Size        Type of Construction        Date last tested

_____

_____

_____

11. HAZARDOUS MATERIALS PRESENT ON PROPERTY:

_____

_____

_____

12. IS ELECTRICAL EQUIPMENT (E.G., TRANSFORMERS, LIGHT BALLASTS) ON THE PROPERTY THAT MAY CONTAIN PCBS?

Yes _____    No _____

13. IF THE ANSWER TO #12 IS "YES," IS ANY OF THIS EQUIPMENT LEAKING?

Yes _____    No _____

14. DO ANY OF THE BUILDINGS ON THE SITE CONTAIN ASBESTOS?

Yes _____ No _____

15. IF THE ANSWER TO #14 IS "YES," IS THE ASBESTOS IN APPARENTLY GOOD CONDITION?

Yes _____ No _____

16. LIST THE TYPES OF BUSINESSES BORDERING THE PROPERTY:

Business                         Location

_____

_____

_____

17. HAVE ANY OF THESE NEIGHBORING PROPERTIES HAD A RELEASE OF HAZARDOUS SUBSTANCES OR ANY OTHER ENVIRONMENTAL PROBLEMS?

Yes _____ No _____

18. IF THE ANSWER TO #17 IS "YES," PLEASE DESCRIBE (USE SEPARATE SHEET IF NECESSARY):

_____

_____

_____

19. IS ANY DISPOSAL SITE FOR GARBAGE OR OTHER WASTES LOCATED ON OR WITHIN 2,000 FEET OF THE PROPERTY?

Yes _____ No _____

20. IF THE ANSWER TO #19 IS "YES," PLEASE INDICATE THE
LOCATION AND NATURE OF THE MATERIALS AT THE SITE:

_____

_____

_____

21. LIST EACH LOCATION ON THE PROPERTY WHERE HAZARDOUS
MATERIALS HAVE BEEN AT ANY TIME STORED, TREATED, DISPOSED
OF, OR RELEASED:

Location                          Nature of activity or release

_____

_____

_____

22. HAS ANY NOTICE BEEN ISSUED BY A GOVERNMENT
AGENCY CONCERNING AN INVESTIGATION OF POSSIBLE
CONTAMINATION OF THE PROPERTY OR THE VIOLATION OF ANY
ENVIRONMENTAL LAWS?

Yes _____   No _____

23. IF THE ANSWER TO #22 IS "YES," EXPLAIN THE DATE AND NATURE
OF EACH SUCH NOTICE:

_____

_____

_____

24. PLEASE ATTACH TO THIS QUESTIONNAIRE:

   a.  Construction plans and specifications, if available

   b.  A site layout, if available

   c.  Any environmental study performed on the property

   d.  Any claims or notices concerning environmental conditions on or about the property

   e.  A list of prior owners of the property for the past 50 years

## FORM 2

### Phase 1 Consultant Contract

Whereas _____
[name of investor] ("Investor") requires an expert consultant in connection with its investigation of environmental conditions at _____

_____

[address of property] (the "Property");

Whereas _____ [name of consultant] ("Consultant") has the required expertise and desires to assist Investor in this investigation:

Therefore, Investor and Consultant agree as follows:

Consultant will perform a "Phase 1" preliminary environmental assessment on the Property, which is designed to provide information concerning the possible presence of environmental conditions on the Property that may require investigation of remediation under, or which may violate, federal, state or local statutes, regulations or policies, including the presence of chemical contamination on or under the Property. This assessment will include:

(1) a walk-through inspection of the Property;

(2) examination of historic aerial photographs and other information revealing past uses of and the potential presence of hazardous materials on the Property;

(3) an examination of the records of relevant federal, state or local agencies to determine whether the Property, or locations neighboring the Property, have been placed on a list of contaminated properties, including but not limited to the CERCLIS list, the National Priorities List, and any list of locations with leaking underground storage tanks;

(4) an examination of pertinent government permitting files to determine whether a permit for an underground storage tank, a hazardous waste generator's number, or any other permit for the treatment, storage or disposal of hazardous materials has ever been issued with respect to the Property;

(5) interviews with persons knowledgeable concerning the historic uses of the Property.

Consultant will provide a report to Investor concerning its findings on the above matters within _____ days from the date of this contract.

Consultant scope of work will include any other inquiries required for Investor to qualify as an "innocent purchaser" under the Comprehensive Environmental Responsibility Cleanup and Liability Act.

Consultant shall be paid for its services under this contract at its usual and customary rates, which amount shall not exceed _____.

Consultant will keep the results of its investigations, including its report, confidential and shall not disclose such results or report to any person or entity, including any governmental entity, except as required by law.

Consultant shall not assign this contract to any person or entity without the express consent of Investor.

Investor may cancel this contract at any time, by delivery of written notice to Consultant, or if the notice is oral, upon actual receipt of such notice. Upon such cancellation, Consultant shall be entitled to fees earned up to the time of delivery or receipt of such notice.

Consultant shall perform its services as an independent contractor, and not as an employee of Investor. Consultant shall obtain and maintain worker's compensation insurance in the amount required by the state wherein the Property is located, and general liability and automobile liability insurance in the amount of $1,000,000 per occurrence, which policy shall name Investor as an additional insured.

No waiver by Investor or Consultant of any term of this contract shall be a waiver of any future or other default of any term of this contract. If any portion of this contract is determined to be invalid, the remainder of this contract shall not be affected and shall be enforced to the fullest extent allowed by law.

This contract contains the entire understanding of the parties, and all other agreements or contracts, written or oral, are superseded by this contract. No modification of this contract shall be made, except by a writing executed by all parties to this contract.

Date: _____    _____
                                          [signature of Investor]


                          _____
                                          [signature of Consultant]

# ABOUT THE AUTHOR

Joel S. Moskowitz has been practicing law for 37 years. Between 1970 and 1983, he was a deputy attorney general for the state of California. For two years, he served California's governor as chief of the toxic substance control programs. He was a partner at Gibson, Dunn & Crutcher, one of the largest law firms in the United States, and after that was a founding partner in his own firm. He is currently senior vice president, Business and Regulatory Affairs, with Caruso Affiliated Holdings, a development company headquartered in Los Angeles, California.

Mr. Moskowitz is the author of numerous publications on law and real estate, including *Environmental Liability and Real Property Transactions* (Aspen Publishers).